# 12 Steps to

# Becoming a More

# Organized Mom

# 12 Steps to Becoming a More Organized Mom

### POSITIVE AND PRACTICAL TIPS FOR BUSY MOMS

## LANE P. JORDAN

12 Steps to Becoming a More Organized Mom
© 2006 by Hendrickson Publishers, Inc.
P. O. Box 3473
Peabody, Massachusetts 01961-3473

ISBN-13: 978-1-56563-309-4
ISBN-10: 1-56563-309-1

Except where otherwise noted, Scripture taken from the Holy Bible, New International Version. Copyright © 1973, 1978, 1984 by International Bible Society. Used by permission of Zondervan Bible Publishers. All rights reserved. (Italics in quoted Scriptures is author's emphasis.)

Family Circus cartoons are © Bil Keane, Inc. King Features Syndicate. Used with permission.

*Printed in the United States of America*

*First Printing — July 2006*

Cover Photo Credit: Yellow Dog Productions/The Image Bank/Getty Images. Used with permission.

**Library of Congress Cataloging-in-Publication Data**

Jordan, Lane P.
    12 steps to becoming a more organized mom / Lane P. Jordan.
        p. cm.
    Includes bibliographical references.
    ISBN-13: 978-1-56563-309-4 (alk. paper)
    ISBN-10: 1-56563-309-1 (alk. paper)
    1. Mothers—Religious life. 2. Motherhood—Religious aspects—Christianity. I. Title. II. Title: Twelve steps to becoming a more organized mom.
    BV4529.18.J67 2006
    248.8′431—dc22
                        2006010722

*To the most wonderful daughters in the world,*
*Christi and Grace.*
*Thank you for who you are,*
*and for the blessing of your love, joy, and support.*


*And to my mom,*
*Marilyn S. Powell,*
*who taught me how to be a mom.*
*Thank you!*

# Table of Contents

# Acknowledgements

Whenever I pick up a book to read, the finished product seems to have come together with so little effort. I have learned, however, that this is never the case. It takes a great deal of time, support, and work by many people to pull together and transform an author's thought and experience into something that—hopefully—will be an inspiration to others.

I acknowledge and thank first my editor Patti Law, who inspired, encouraged, and helped me believe I could actually finish this book! Without her help during the editing process, I would not have been able to complete the book on time. Patti, thank you for caring about my work and for all your support and help.

I also wish to thank Hendrickson Publishers, who asked me to write this book, and Sara Scott, who helped get this project going and completed. Thank you for your trust in me and for your desire to help mothers.

I am grateful to Dan Penwell, who published my first book and encouraged me to continue writing. Dan, you are an inspiration to me.

Many thanks also to my prayer partners. Without prayer, we can do nothing! Thank you for being there for me, and for lifting up this book to God in prayer.

But most of all, I give thanks to my Father, His Son, Jesus Christ, and His wonderful Holy Spirit, who worked in me for His glory. You gave me the strength to "press on toward the goal . . . for which God has called me" (Philippians 3:14). Thank you.

# Introduction

*I* remember coming home from the hospital with my first baby, a precious daughter dressed in pink and oh, so sweet! Because of complications from a C-section, I had been in the hospital for eight days. I was very ready to get away from all the hospital interruptions and back to my own bed for some much-needed sleep. I was also looking forward to wearing my beautiful new robe and rocking my content, sleeping baby as I gazed out the window in new-motherhood bliss.

That vision was shattered in only a few hours, because for the next five months this gift from above had colic! Forget the beautiful robe. I was lucky just to get dressed each day or have anything to eat. My dreams of celestial motherhood quickly faded as I cried them away.

Have you had wonderful expectations and dreams of yourself as a mother, only to have them crash and burn before your very eyes? Well, if you have, you are not alone. Having my first baby was like having an earthquake shake my life from beginning to end, and I hadn't just fallen off the turnip truck either. I was twenty-nine years old, a college graduate, and working in our family business. I had been married for almost six years, and we owned our own home. We had decorated the nursery, written thank-you notes for gifts, and prepared the gifts for use. Quitting work and taking care of a baby was going to be a piece of cake. Or so I thought!

My problem was that I had temporarily forgotten that life isn't like the movies or the cover of a women's magazine. Life comes in all shapes and sizes, and it changes from one moment to the next. For some of you, the birth of your baby and the first few years that followed were wonderful. (Perhaps your earthquake will occur later, in the teenage years.) For others of you, sickness or hospitalization was part of your pregnancy; not to mention continuing health problems brought on by a difficult birth.

Now more than ever, we moms struggle under the constant demands and stress of motherhood. The balancing act we try to maintain in order to fulfill all our roles as moms—cook and snack specialist, nanny and babysitter, maid, twenty-four-hour chauffeur, sibling referee, teacher of all subjects, nurse, librarian, veterinarian, Bible teacher, homeroom mother, Girl Scout leader, camping expert, curer of hurts with a single kiss, expert at managing financial and time stress that come from working outside the home—is literally mind boggling. To add to the demands, many of us are not living near our extended families, who in the past were a great source of help and support to mothers.

But there is one thing I know for sure: we have a God who knows exactly what is going on in our lives and hearts every day, both the good days and the bad. We have a God who understands the struggles and hardships that are so much a part of the "daily-ness" of motherhood. He knows that the mundane aspects of raising children can cause us to become so tired. He also knows that when we are most exhausted, we begin to doubt who we are, what we are doing, and whether we are accomplishing anything at all worthwhile.

This is when, as we trust in Him, God reminds us that He wouldn't have called us to be His servants without equipping us for the challenge. Our "success" as mothers will never have anything to do with our *own* abilities, our *own* strengths, or our *own* skills. Our success as mothers depends completely on God's presence in our lives, our dependence on Him, and our willingness to allow the Lord to fill us with His supernatural joy, strength, and wisdom each day. If we don't have a clear sense of our God-given purpose or mission as moms, we will only flounder as we make our way down the road of motherhood. We become strong and successful because God gives us the grace, wisdom, and patience we need. Remembering this one fact, that God is taking care of you, will relieve the pressure of trying to be the "perfect mom."

I know that only two things will last for all eternity: God's Word and God's people. God has blessed me with the joy of serving Him through raising my daughters, and my goal is to raise them on the foundation of His Word. I can look to the world for guidance in making the parental decisions that confront me every day, or I can look to God for this. Being earthly-minded or God-centered are the two choices set before all of us. I choose to be God-centered, and to have the peace that passes all human understanding (Philippians 4:7).

I pray that as you read this book you will be encouraged, motivated, and strengthened to run the race and press on toward the goal God has placed before you as a mother. I am on the same path you are, struggling daily with the hardships and joys of raising children. My prayer is that this book will somehow help you see above and beyond the daily grind of diapers and dishes to the kingdom of heaven. God is so faithful! He will never leave you. He simply asks you to give Him your burdens, so He can take care of them and give you rest. He promises to do more than you or I could ever hope or imagine. That's our heavenly Father, the best example of the way we are to parent our own children.

Believe me when I say that I have gone through almost everything most of you moms are going through or have been through. When I was taking care of my colicky baby, I don't think I slept or ate for months. I had to move across the country three times in eleven years. (Trust me, if you have never done this, count your blessings!) I feared for both our finances and our future when my husband lost two jobs. I endured the agonizing pain of rejection when I found out my husband had not been true to his vows and our marriage of twenty-five years came to an end. I had to watch my beautiful daughters go through the pain and scarring of these events, and I know that apart from God's hand they might never have healed. I have experienced depression so deep that all I could do was lie in bed. As a single mom, I wondered if I could ever get a job again, after not working out of the home for over eighteen years. I felt insecure and old and I couldn't stop crying, but at the same time I was trying to be strong for my daughters. I have cared for a loved one with cancer, and I personally have dealt with an illness that at times causes my whole body to ache and lose movement. I have lived in cities where I did not know a soul and have been overwhelmed by the loneliness that accompanied raising small children without any support.

I share my story here only as a way of saying that my purpose in writing this book is *not* to suggest to any of you moms that I have "arrived." Believe me, I struggle every day just to get my contacts in! I have not, nor will I ever, arrive at that place where one receives a gold-plated award for perfection. But God has called me to encourage, to motivate, and to love moms. You have a harder job than any Fortune 500 CEO, because society isn't cheering you on. Well, I am! The purpose of this book is to help you become organized in every aspect of your life, so that you can experience God's love and care more deeply than you ever thought possible and pass that relationship on to your children.

This book provides tips, ideas, and ways to help you identify where you are right now and where you want to grow as a mom. We will look at how to manage time; plan and prepare meals; care for your emotional, mental, and spiritual health; discipline your children; and tend to your relationships with your husband and friends. At the end of the book there are resources you can turn to for additional help.

At this point you may be asking, "Why get organized?" My response is that, when we have our "act together," we experience less stress, have more time, and acquire a new outlook on life. These positive attitudes provide the best example to our children of the way to live and follow God in our lives. As the apostle

Paul said, "One thing I do: Forgetting what is behind and straining toward what is ahead, I press on toward the goal to win the prize for which God has called me heavenward in Christ Jesus" (Philippians 3:13–14). These verses will be the main theme developed throughout this book. God has given us the gift of life, and our heavenward call is to raise up these precious gifts to the glory of God.

You may be married or single. You may live in your own home, an apartment, or with your parents. You may be working full time, part time, or at home. Regardless of what your situation is, you are still a mom! Every chapter in this book is written expressly for you and only you. I have been a married mom and a single mom, a working mom and a stay-at-home mom. I have lived through years of babies, children, adolescents, teens, college, and marriage. This book is relevant to all moms at every stage in life. Even grandmothers will enjoy reading this book.

Moms, forget all your past mistakes! There is so much God wants to give you right now. He says that He will give back to you "the years that the swarming locust has eaten" (Joel 2:25 NASB). Seek God, obey His calling, and press on toward the goal He has given you, to raise your children for His glory. Get ready to become the best you can be for God and your family.

Moms, the best is yet to come!

# Step 1
## Seek God First

**"Seek first his kingdom
and his righteousness . . ."
—Matthew 6:33**

eing a mom can be one of the most complex occupations a person can undertake. From the long list of responsibilities in the job description, to the emotional highs and lows, to the push and pull of every segment of society, the challenges are enough to make many of us moms want to throw up our hands in defeat! But we don't. We don't because we are resilient, strong, and like the Energizer Bunny: we just keep going, going, going!

As you begin working with this book to become a more organized mom, I want you to understand that there has to be something else—an extra catalyst—that makes the difference between success and failure as a mom. I believe that the "something else" is the power and strength of the Lord in our lives. For this reason, the first step in becoming a more organized mom is to seek the Lord daily in your life.

Because of all the different hats we moms have to wear, all the decisions we have to make, and all the answers we have to provide throughout our children's lives, it doesn't take long before we begin to realize that we aren't "superheroes"; we're only human. But when we tap into God as the "power source" in our lives, we obtain God's wisdom and God's Spirit, who gives us the graciousness and gentleness that a mom must have. Galatians 5:22–23 lists the wonderful attributes that can be ours when we walk with the Lord: "The fruit of the Spirit is love, joy, peace, patience, kindness, goodness, faithfulness, gentleness and self-control." When we put God first in our lives, through committing ourselves to His truths, the fruits of the Holy Spirit that are so necessary for being a successful mom are given to us.

Along with receiving the fruits of the Holy Spirit, when we put God first, we also receive His great wisdom, simply for the asking: "If any of you lacks wisdom, he should ask God, who gives generously to all without finding fault, and it will be given to him" (James 1:5). I would not last one day as a mom if I couldn't go to the throne of grace and ask God to help me with all I need to know. The wisdom of God provides the answer for every problem you will ever face. God is the One who created everything, and He can take care of every problem we have.

I have often wondered what it would have been like to see God create the heavens and the earth. Did He first sit down with pen and paper to design it, before speaking His words of creation? How much time did it take for God to decide what would come first—water or land, sea creatures or fowl, trees or grass? In Proverbs 8 we are given a glimpse of these beginnings. The chapter concerns Wisdom, how the wise pay heed to "her" and how the Lord created Wisdom. My hope is that you will see how important God's wisdom is to you as a mom.

> The LORD formed me from the beginning, before he created anything else. I was appointed in ages past, at the very first, before the earth began. I was born before the oceans were created, before the springs bubbled forth their waters. Before the mountains and the hills were formed, I was born—before he had made the earth and fields and the first handfuls of soil.
>
> I was there when he established the heavens, when he drew the horizon on the oceans. I was there when he set the clouds above,

*when he established the deep fountains of the earth. I was there when he set the limits of the seas, so they would not spread beyond their boundaries. And when he marked off the earth's foundations, I was the architect at his side. I was his constant delight, rejoicing always in his presence. And how happy I was with what he created—his wide world and all the human family!*

*And so, my children, listen to me, for happy are all who follow my ways. Listen to my counsel and be wise. Don't ignore it.*

*Happy are those who listen to me, watching for me daily at my gates, waiting for me outside my home! For whoever finds me finds life and wins approval from the LORD. But those who miss me have injured themselves. All who hate me love death.* (*Proverbs 8:22–36* NLT)

This passage teaches us that, before God spoke anything into existence, He first created Wisdom, and with her He created all that exists in the heavens and earth. So, before *we* begin to do or make anything in order to become more organized moms, we need to do all we can to obtain God's wisdom.

God gives us another word of help for everything that comes our way: "Seek first his kingdom and his righteousness, and all these things will be given to you as well" (Matthew 6:33). What types of "things," you might ask? Everything you need to know, everything you need to do, and everything you need to have in your life. In other words, God wants us first to come to know Him and experience His love. Then, as we walk in the nearness of His presence each day, He will give us the things we need.

This is why the first step in becoming a more organized mom is to seek God before everything else. Just about anyone can write a book to motivate you to straighten up and become organized in your life, but what is the purpose behind all this? Just to be more organized? No, the real benefit and goal of organizing our lives is to know God and serve Him fully, in whatever capacity He calls us. Since you are a mother, parenting is one of the major tasks God has called you to do. Remember, moms, "your labor in the Lord is not in vain" (1 Corinthians 15:58).

*Unbelief puts our circumstances between us and God.*
*Faith puts God between us and our circumstances.*

—F. B. Meyer

 # Personal Inventory

Before providing tips, personal stories, and advice from experts, I want to give you time to think about where you are with this first step. This will be time well spent because, when you see where you are as opposed to where you want to be, then deciding how you will get there becomes clearer and easier. Take a few moments now to answer the following questions about yourself. You are planting seeds here, seeds that will grow as you read the rest of this chapter. When you make your "Plan of Action" at the end of the chapter, you'll be harvesting the fruit of your planting. Let's get digging!

1. What does it mean to you to "seek God first"? How would you put this idea into your own words?

   _____

   _____

2. Who do you know that does this well? What is it about this person that you admire?

   _____

   _____

3. In your own life, how are you seeking God and making Him first?

   _____

   _____

4. What are some things your children are learning about God from the way you live your life, the good and not so good?

_____

_____

5. Name three areas of your life where you want to begin seeking God first before everything else. Then number these in order of priority.

#_____   _____

#_____   _____

#_____   _____

---

*Your attitude determines the state of the world you live in. It is the foundation for every success and every failure you have had and will have. Your attitude will make you or break you.*

—Mark Victor Hansen,
author of *Chicken Soup for the Soul*

---

 *Everybody Wins!*

When my first daughter was just a toddler, I remember hearing how important reading is to a child's development and especially how important reading Scripture and Bible stories is to their spiritual development. I asked a friend whose husband owned a Christian bookstore if she had any suggestions as to what might be age-appropriate for my daughter, and she and I picked out some great books. (This was twenty-five years ago, when the market for Christian books was almost nonexistent.) After I bought the books, I realized that I needed to come up with a plan at home to help me actually *use* them. I found that, if I put the books in a basket beside my daughter's rocking chair, it would remind me to read them to her.

From this one tiny step grew my daily ritual of reading with my children before naptime and bedtime. Reading together became a great time for bonding, a time to communicate, touch, and understand one another. As my girls grew up, so did the level of the books we read. We went from picture books and Bible stories to chapter books and devotionals. They never fussed about going to bed because I just said, "Run upstairs and pick out the book you want me to read!" If I hadn't been organized, I wouldn't have had the time or energy to seek out buying the books and place them where we would use them; I would have missed out on many wonderful years of quality time with my daughters. The time we spent reading together was a very tangible benefit of being organized, and everybody won!

When we aren't very organized as moms, our children suffer. Some of you are struggling, and that is why you are reading this book. Please don't become overwhelmed or feel guilty! I still struggle every day with my routines. I have to work hard just to get up on time and begin the day well. We all have weaknesses, but we also have strengths. As you and I put the Lord first in our lives and begin to pray and work at becoming more organized, we will begin to see great changes taking place in our homes. Everyone wins when we become organized, and the first thing to organize is our relationship with God.

# *What I've Learned*

Having raised two daughters, I've learned that when I put God first—before all my other relationships and concerns—I have a greater sense of peace, patience, and love for others. I also am less judgmental, critical, frustrated, or depressed about life. Then, when the plumbing breaks while I'm cooking dinner for company, a flat tire halts our trip to the store, an earache keeps me up all night, or my hormones are flying high, these things don't push me over the cliff of despair. When I put God first, my perspective on life's interruptions becomes so much more realistic and balanced. I *want* to remain positive, to see the glass as totally full instead of empty! A mom who focuses on God first can only instill great things in her children.

So, it's time to ask yourself some questions. In general, are you a positive or negative person? How do your words come across to others? Proverbs 18:21 says, "The tongue has the power of life and death." Is your tongue one that blesses or curses? Do you "bless our Lord and Father, and with it [the tongue] . . . curse men, who have been made in the likeness of God" (James 3:9 NASB)? Are your actions negative and disruptive? Do you slam doors, speed in the car, yell at your children, and exhibit other types of negative behavior? What are your children learning from your life? Let me admit right away that I am guilty of all of the above. It isn't that I want to be negative, disruptive, or reckless, but sometimes life becomes overwhelming and I get stressed and out of order.

When I was a teenager, I committed my life to God through a wonderful organization called Young Life. But when I went to college, I forgot to put God first. After a few years of bad decisions and crises, I began to seek God again. Wow, what changes came over my life! My thoughts, my words, my goals, and my values all began to be more positive and life affirming. As I grew up in the Lord, I became more the person I wanted to be.

Moms, God gives us this encouragement:

*Do not be anxious about anything [that means don't worry!], but in everything, by prayer and petition, with thanksgiving, present your requests to God. And the peace of God, which transcends all understanding, will guard your hearts and your minds in Christ Jesus. (Philippians 4:6–7)*

These verses teach us that *every day* we have to fall on our faces before the Lord and admit that we can't do anything without His help—and mean it! This is what God is waiting for. He already knows we need Him, for *He created us to be in a personal relationship with Him.* But He waits for us to hear His voice, follow His lead, and totally depend on Him.

At this point you might be thinking, "But, Lane, you don't know my circumstances. You have no idea how difficult it is to be the mother of a disabled child or a critically ill child, or to be a single mom, or to live from paycheck to paycheck, or to be in an abusive marriage." No, dear sister, I do not know all of the trials that many of you are going through. But God knows, and that is all that matters. Seek God first, Jesus said, and all these things . . .

When you seek God first, you begin to see yourself and your circumstances from God's perspective. Remember Job? He didn't understand what was happening when everything he owned was destroyed, his children were killed, and sores broke out all over his body (Job 1–2). Job wrestled with the reason all of these things happened to him, especially since he loved and obeyed God. But he was trying to understand his situation and his suffering from a human standpoint, not from God's perspective (Job 1:6–12; 2:1–7). He could not know or understand that eventually God would restore all that had been taken from him (Job 42:12–17).

God's perspective is vital if we are to understand the meaning of difficult circumstances. Bad times can overwhelm us. If we see only our immediate circumstances, our understanding of life and God becomes distorted. We might come to think that "God doesn't love me" or "God is not fair." Or, we might begin to question God's love and His wisdom, saying, "God, why didn't you stop me?" or "Why did this happen, Lord?" Sometimes we ask the wrong questions, and end up with wrong answers.

Ask God to show you His perspective on your circumstances in a way you can understand. When you face difficult or confusing circumstances, the Spirit of God will reveal the truth to you and help you understand your situation. Remember that it takes patience to wait on the Holy Spirit, and you may have to adjust your life as you wait to see what God does in and through you in this difficulty. As you wait, trust, and obey God you will begin to experience Him as you never have before.

When I am in a difficult situation, it helps me to remember other women who have endured great trials. Joni Eareckson Tada became paralyzed from the neck down after diving into shallow water, but she is now living a life of great victory and ministry to others. Her response to bad circumstances was to trust the Lord. She is a wonderful example and an inspiration to me. Helen Keller, another woman who inspires me, once said, "I thank God for my handicaps, for through them, I have found myself, my work, and my God." Here is a woman who couldn't see, hear, or speak well, yet her faith in God was unwavering! She learned the secret of putting God first in her life, and her reward was a life of deep joy and peace.

 *Try This . . .*

- ☀ Moms, are you looking for tips on *how* to put God first in your life? Try one of these!

- ☀ Set aside time each day (when the baby is napping, the kids are in school, you're on your lunch break, etc.) to read and reflect on Scripture without interruption. You might read a chapter a day in the Gospels, write down every time Jesus uses an image to describe our relationship with God, then meditate on the implications of this image for your life.

- Try reading one chapter of Proverbs a day. Since there are thirty-one chapters in the book of Proverbs and there are often thirty-one days in a month, this will give you a month's worth of great reading.

- Join (or start!) a moms' group that is connected with a church or Christian organization, so that you can be with other moms who want to follow God as they raise their children.

- Become involved in a Sunday school class at your church. (I have made lifetime friends this way.)

 # Set a Good Example

Moms, one of the best things you can do for your children is to set a good example for them. Children learn more by example than by words. There is no better way to set a good example for your children than by seeking God first in your life. When your children see you pray, read and study the Bible, go to Bible studies and Sunday school classes, and (especially) hear you talk about the Lord as you go about your day, they see and experience what living a life of faith really means and looks like. The choices your children make and the values they adopt will likewise be based on *their* relationship with the Lord. I pray that as you read through this book, you will be blessed with a vision of the way you can seek God first that will be contagious to your children!

"Make me be good. And if You don't get
through to me the first time, please keep
tryin' 'til I answer."

 *Stress Busters!*

As you begin this journey of becoming a more organized mom, I want to offer you some suggestions on how to reduce stress in your life. The lack of time, energy, or focus to seek God can be very stressful. Below are a few things that help me with daily stress:

* Ask your husband to put the kids to bed while you disappear for a long bubble bath with candles and music that directs your soul toward God.

* Take a private walk in the woods. Reflect on the way God is with you in the beauty and quiet stillness, making "all things new." Speak your hopes, fears, and frustrations out loud to God.

Create a place in the house where you can meet with God *every day.* Place your Bible, devotional, notebook or journal, a pen, and a highlighter there. You will sense God's presence in new ways as you meet with Him there each day. It's amazing the way a little thing like a regular meeting place can transform our relationship with God.

# Bringing It Home

The goal of this book is to encourage and help you become the best mom you can be. That doesn't mean you have to be perfect. None of us will ever be perfect. But hopefully, throughout this book you will pick up tips that will help you spend more time on the important tasks and less on the time-wasters. By focusing on becoming a more organized person, you will become a more organized mom!

We need to put God first in our words and actions.

We need to ask God for wisdom.

We need to apply to our lives what we learn from God's Word.

There are so many benefits that come from putting God first in our lives. We enjoy the beautiful fruits of the Spirit: love, joy, peace, patience, kindness, goodness, faithfulness, gentleness, and self-control. These qualities are crucial for successfully raising children. We are also given access to God's great wisdom, which will help us in the many decisions we have to make as mothers. When we seek God first in our lives, He promises that "all these things will be given to you as well" (Matthew 6:33). We become less frustrated, critical, and despondent about life, and, most of all, we come to know our Lord more fully and deeply.

For me, I knew I needed a method that would help me teach my children to seek God for themselves. I was already having a devotional time with the Lord each day, and He led me to search for books to read to my daughters before bedtime, which ended up being priceless moments shared with my girls. As you become more organized in this first step of putting God first in your life, you, too, will experience benefits to your family.

---

*The secret of getting ahead is getting started.*
*The secret of getting started is breaking your complex*
*overwhelming tasks into small manageable tasks,*
*and then starting on the first one.*

—Mark Twain

---

 ## Plan of Action

In our first step toward becoming a more organized mom we have focused on the need to "Seek God First" with all our hearts. Now it's time for the rubber to meet the road and ask the question, where do *you* want to be in your relationship with God? How do you want to get there, with God's help? Look back at your response to Question #5 in the "Personal Inventory" section for this chapter. Do you still agree with what you wrote and the priority you gave your three ideas? If you do, then complete the sentence below by writing in your #1 choice. If your thoughts have changed since reading the chapter, write your new first priority below.

With God's help, I want to _____.

I think I will have to change _____ in order to make this happen. I'm ready to step out in faith with God and make this change so that I can put God and His wisdom first in my life.

Moms, I want more than anything for you to be able to put together the pieces of your life. Some of you are already working at this. Others are frantically wondering how one even begins. The next step, after seeking God first, is to say to yourself, "Now is the time to work on becoming more organized, because I want to be a more together mom, who can minister to, develop, and grow my children the best I possibly can." This is the attitude that will make it happen.

Remember, we can't change what we don't acknowledge. So mom, what are the most disorganized parts of your life? It might be the whole house, a specific room, or a closet. It could be papers and mail stacked in every corner. It could be your family time, or your relationship with your husband. Your most disorganized part could also be time itself, if you find yourself running in all directions but never catching up. (We'll tackle the challenge of time management in the next chapter.)

Once you have written down the few areas that are most disorganized in your life, break down one of these into small, manageable parts. For example, perhaps the area that is most in need of organization is your garage. Write down that the first area of your life that you want to organize is the garage. Look for a time on your calendar when you can address this project and jot it down on the calendar. Survey the area and decide if you will need to buy anything to organize that garage, such as shelves, plastic bins for better storage, hooks for hanging bikes and yard equipment, etc. Shelves, hooks, and plastic bins can keep your whole house organized and clutter free.

Now, take everything out of the garage. I know it's a daunting task, but it has to be done. As you take out the items, place them in three different stacks: items for a garage sale, items for the trash, and items that need to be repaired or placed in bins with labels. With everything out of the garage, now is the time to sweep and/or hose it out. If you can afford it, paint the garage floor with special concrete paint or a special sealer; this will make a huge difference in the appearance of your garage and will also keep down dust.

Now it's time to store the items that need to be in the garage. Perhaps you have already placed shelves there. (We bought large closets so that each person had a place for shoes, sport equipment, and toys.) If you have an activity that needs to be done in the garage, such as carpentry or crafts, mark off a special zone for this so others won't put their things there. By the time you have thrown away, given away, or sold most of the items, you will have room for your cars and the important items you want to keep safe and dry. Label all boxes and plastic storage bins so that you can find what you want when you need it.

This is just one example of how to begin organizing a part of your life. As we go along, I will share other tips that can help you with your organizational trouble spots. Remember to enjoy the journey, get excited, don't worry, and expect great things from God!

# Step 2
## Manage Your Time

**"There is a time for everything, and a season
for every activity under heaven."
—Ecclesiastes 3:1**

*I* believe that the most important commodity we have in our
short span of life is time. It is also the most elusive. You can't see it,
touch it, or feel it. And it has no compassion for those who need
more of it or for those who have too much of it. Time is valuable,
because if we use it wisely, then we can accomplish great things for
ourselves, our families, and our world. If we don't use it wisely, we
could fail at everything we attempt to do.

How many times have you heard a mom say in frustration,
"Who's got the time?" It's such a loaded question. Just having
someone ask me this question causes me to feel stressed. "No one
has the time for *anything* anymore!" I want to reply. And, after
all the things we are expected to do—carpooling, meals, laundry, errands, doctor appointments, grocery shopping, birthday
parties, school supplies, soccer games, ballet lessons, ballet recitals,
music lessons, PTA meetings, Brownies, homeroom mom, housework, feeding the pets, taking the pets to the vet, cleaning up after
the pets, paying bills, writing cards, sending packages, planting
flowers, helping with homework (all right, *doing* the homework!),

keeping in touch with your mom or his mom, finishing up your Bible study lesson, crawling in bed with your little one who is up at 2 a.m., remembering to set the alarm early to take your tenth-grader to morning band practice, waking up, this time in your own bed but having forgotten your name—just remember, your name is Mom!

Some of you may be reading this list and laughing because you've had days when *all* of the above activities had to be done on the same day! Yes, there is never enough time for everything we need or want to do. One thing I have come to understand is that I have to *make* the time to sort out my priorities, so that time works *for* me. When I don't plan and schedule and organize my time, time *rules* me. Let's figure out where your time is being spent right now.

---

## Most Common Time-Wasters

- ☀ *attempting to do too much at once*
- ☀ *being unable to say "No"*
- ☀ *making unrealistic estimates about time*
- ☀ *procrastinating*
- ☀ *trying to do everything yourself*
- ☀ *being disorganized*
- ☀ *focusing on unnecessary details*
- ☀ *failing to write things down*

---

# Personal Inventory

Everyone handles time differently. Some of us love to be spontaneous while others like to plan way ahead; most of us fall somewhere in between. Take a few minutes to think about the way you manage—or don't manage!—your days. Be honest with yourself. Remember, you can't change what you don't first acknowledge.

1. In general, how do you prefer to handle your time?

    1___2___3___4___5___6___7___8___9___10

    I like to be                                     I like to
    be spontaneous                          make plans

2. If you had an extra hour every day to do something with your family, what would you do? Explain your answer.

    _____

    _____

3. Think of something you have wanted to do for yourself but haven't had (or made) time to do. What are some things you could change that would allow you to have time to pursue this interest of yours?

    _____

    _____

4. If you could change one thing about the way you manage your time, what would it be?

    _____

    _____

5. Who do you know that manages time well? What question might you ask her in order to learn how she does this so well?

_____

_____

6. Name three areas in your life where you want to learn to manage time better. Then number these in order of priority.

#____  _____

#____  _____

#____  _____

---

*It has been wisely said, "Sow a thought, reap an action. Sow an action, reap a habit. Sow a habit, reap character. Sow character, reap a destiny." Our choices matter. A key component of our choices is the way we spend our time.*

—Our Daily Bread

---

 # Everybody Wins!

As I mentioned earlier, when we organize the twenty-four hours of time we are given each day, we gain so much. We gain more time for our chores, our jobs, our hobbies. As moms, I believe that the most important thing we gain when we organize our time is the growth and development of our family. Children spell the word *Love* with these letters: *T.I.M.E.* They don't understand the concept of time, nor the constraints that rule our lives. What they do understand is that when they want you, they want you now! No matter how unfair this seems, it doesn't alter the fact that children want their moms to be available when they need them.

It is so that moms will have more time for their families that I wrote this book, because if we aren't organized with our time, our families suffer—big time. Eating together, reading together, teaching and instilling spiritual truths about life won't just happen; we have to be intentional about making time for these things. If we manage our time well, then we become more giving and less selfish, and the payoffs in the future are enormous! This doesn't mean that single moms or working moms need to feel guilty. Not at all! It only means that you have to organize your life that much more tightly. Our children know when we are sincere; when you try to be there for your children on a consistent basis, they know it.

When I was going through my divorce and was so depressed, I know I wasn't the best mom, but my daughters knew I only wanted the best for them. They *knew* they were first in my life because I showed them through the way I used my time. We were able to get through that very difficult season in such a way that everybody could win in the end.

 ## *What I've Learned*

One thing I have learned in using time to my advantage is that we have to do those things that *must* be done first. One of the biggest challenges a mom faces is developing the ability to finish her work even when there are constant interruptions. When I was newly married, a good friend explained to me how the women of her family did their chores as quickly as they could in the mornings, so that after lunch they would have free time for crafts, hobbies, or watching their favorite soap operas!

When I became a stay-at-home mom just before the birth of my first child, I began to implement this method of time management. I found that it worked great, because it gave me the motivation to do chores quickly, whether I felt like it or not. I was able to work on projects I wanted to do, take a nap, paint, do needlework, or read in the afternoons because my daily chores were mostly finished. As I progressed in becoming a "domestic engineer," I used this concept to devise a fun and easy plan. The principle of "work first then play" seems like a sacrifice, but in reality it produced great benefits for me and my children. They learned at an early age that chores have to be done, and the sooner you take care of them, the sooner you can relax and have fun.

I eventually refined this method into what I call "The 5-Minute Quick-Clean." Each morning before I head out the door, I quickly go through the bedrooms, picking up dirty clothes, collecting trash, turning off lights and curling irons, and straightening up a bit. When my children were little, I gave them a light trash can or duster and made them part of my team. Young children love to help mom, and teaching them chores at a young age is imperative—they will resist doing chores if you wait until they're older. I made the chores fun by telling them to race through the house to see how fast we could accomplish our quick-clean, so that the rest of the day we could do whatever we wanted. In the evening, before they went to bed, we would check over the living areas of our home. We turned off lights, plumped pillows, collected newspapers, put out shoes and schoolbooks, unloaded the dishwasher, set the table for breakfast, made lunches, and turned off the computer or TV. That way, when we woke up the next morning the downstairs was already straightened and clutter free. What a great way to begin the day!

## Try This...

If you've never been one to organize your time yourself but have let your children's and husband's needs and your boss's demands "choose" for you, then it's time to take back that responsibility—for the sake of your own sanity and self-esteem. Try these tips and see if the next few weeks don't go more smoothly for everyone.

Step 1:    Begin with a calendar, on your computer, handheld computer, or desk calendar. I recommend electronic calendars because you and your husband can share the same calendar and update it easily in order to know what is going on with one another. Enter all your family's appointments, events, meetings, rehearsals, etc. You might try color-coding each category for quick reference.

Step 2:    Make a list of everything you *have* to do in the coming week—including the laundry (trust me on this: if you plan a time to do it, it takes less time). Put these items on your calendar, including *when* they must be done; estimate how much time will be required for each item.

Step 3:    Notice the open blocks of time on your calendar. Be encouraged! This means there is hope for doing more of what you really *want* to do.

Step 4:    Now make a list of everything you *want* to do that same week. This could be as simple as taking a bubble bath, or going for a walk, or talking with a long-distance friend by phone. It could also be enjoying a special hobby or putting down on paper a dream you've had. Write it down on your list. Then find open spaces on your calendar and begin to schedule the things you really want to do. By placing them on your calendar, you will be less likely to waste time and more able to do what you want to do.

Remember to stay flexible. Just because you plan your time doesn't mean a doctor's appointment, unexpected guests, or a flat tire won't change all your well-made plans. But at least you have a workable framework for your days and weeks, which will eventually become your way of life.

*More Ways to Save Time . . .*

- ❀ Do all your errands in one day. This saves on gas money as well as time. And, if you do your errands at off-peak times (bank on days other than the first or fifteenth of the month, or on Fridays; grocery shop in the mornings or after dinner; do car repairs at the beginning of the week), you'll get finished much more quickly.

- ❀ Draw a map of your grocery store. Your map will remind you where certain items are located and help you organize your shopping list according to where items are located in the store. No more backtracking!

- ❀ When scheduling doctor appointments, ask for the first morning or first afternoon appointment and you won't have to wait as long.

- ❀ Pick a pharmacy that is located in the grocery store where you shop to save an extra trip.

- ❀ Look for coupons for everything. Of course this saves money, but collecting coupons also reminds me of the items I need, so I won't forget them as easily when shopping.

- ❀ Keep reading materials or projects in your car or purse at all times. This is the way I keep up with my periodicals, letters from ministries, Bible study lessons, etc. I pull them out whenever I'm waiting for one of my children, at a doctor's office, or having my car serviced.

※ Don't procrastinate! Procrastination is "living your life with the brakes on." Procrastination leads to worry, and worry can cause more stress than actually doing what you are trying to avoid.

※ Delegate responsibilities. We cannot, nor should we, do everything for our family members. Think through your list of chores and begin to delegate them to your husband and children. Even little ones can set the table or unload the dishwasher.

※ Create a "Command Post" in your home. Every successful corporation has an upper management staff that runs the company. Your home is like a corporation, and you are the Chief Operating Officer. If you have a built-in desk in your kitchen, you already have a command post. If not, create a workstation with desk accessories, your calendar, note paper, address book, telephone, etc., and run your family's schedule from there.

※ Organize the mail and paperwork in your home. Have a file for everything: each child, activities, medical records, passports, bills, taxes, etc. Keeping files is one of the easiest ways to organize all your paperwork.

※ Handle your mail—and e-mail—once. If you open, sort, and respond to your mail all at one time, you will save *huge* amounts of time. Your motto: Touch it once.

※ Remember the magic word: *simplify.* One way that the Enemy distracts us is by offering us too much to do, all in the name of "good works." Please don't fall into his trap! If you don't have time to play with your children and husband, and to keep up with your chores, then perhaps you are involved in too many outside activities.

*Tips for Planning Your Future . . .*

For those of you who feel good about the way you plan your week but want some tips for organizing your time next year, try these suggestions. On your master calendar set aside an area where you can post notes to yourself. For example, in August post a note to remind you and your family to set goals for the new school year; in January remind yourselves to set goals for the new year. I highly recommend that everyone gather together and write a family mission statement and goals each year. Then, when your children are old enough, they can create personal goals for themselves in academics, sports, ministry, music, or whatever and wherever God leads them. This is also an excellent time for you and your husband to help them discern God's direction in their lives.

Remember, the purpose of this book—for you to become more organized—is so you can become the mom God has called you to be. Organizing your time better can improve every aspect of your life. God promises to give us His wisdom, which is the only truth and the only way to become successful as a mom. As you set about organizing your time, set aside time each day to be with God, and your life will have purpose, joy, and meaning.

 # Set a Good Example

One of the most important ways we teach our children is by our example. We can *tell* them to do something, but they will get the message much faster if they *see* us do it! Think of all the ways you can be a good example for your children: stay calm in emergencies, speak kindly to others, handle your duties responsibly. When they see you do these things, they will incorporate your principles into their own lives. Of course, realizing that everything we do is being mirrored and copied by our children can create great pressure on parents! So, remember to commit your life to the

Lord daily, asking Him to lead you as you lead your children. Paul offers this admonition, "Be very careful, then, how you live—not as unwise but as wise, making the most of every opportunity" (Ephesians 5:15–16).

 ## Stress Busters!

Trying to set a good example for your children on a daily basis can be very stressful, so you need to have some fun and downtime every day. When I was a new mother, the highlight of my day was going to the mailbox! I was so overwhelmed by caring for this new baby and trying to keep up my normal routine that I was overjoyed to get out of the house even for that brief moment. Trust me, all you new moms, your daily routines will change as you adjust to this new person in your life. Learn to relax, be flexible, and understand what truly is and is not important each day. Try one of these stress-relieving ideas and see if you don't experience a lift.

- Declare this Saturday "Anything-Goes Day!" Let the kids get up when they want, eat what they want for breakfast, and wear what they want for play. Give each child a chance to choose one thing you will all do together that day. Children love to feel like they are in charge, and you will love that you don't have to make them do anything for a day.

- The next time your children have a school holiday make it an "Upside-down Day." Do things in a different order throughout the day. For instance, eat breakfast food for dinner!

- Choose one night a week to be "Family Night," when you eat pizza and carrot sticks and play games or watch a family-friendly movie. This is time with family members only.

- If you have little children, try staying home every other day. This routine will give you more energy and more time to get chores done. It also will give you more one-on-one time with each of your children. You'll experience less stress and more time to read and play. You might stay in your pajamas longer on the days when you stay at home!

- Every morning plan one nice thing to do for yourself that day. This may sound easy, but it's not. You will be amazed how much better you feel about all the things you do for others when you do something special for yourself each day.

 *Bringing It Home*

We expend a lot of energy struggling with time, trying to get more of it and trying to make it work for *us*. Those of you who have already become successful at managing time will have an easier time managing your role as a mom. But for the majority of us, becoming good stewards of our time often presents a challenge. Below are some of the main points to take from this chapter:

- Be diligent about managing your time, as part of becoming a good steward.

- Plan and put to good use the time you save; that is, spend more time with your family.

- Show (and tell) your children how to use time wisely.

Some of you may be thinking that this is all well and good, but you just don't think you'll ever get a grip on your time. Well, as a way of motivating you to try to make time work for you, let's look at some of the benefits you might enjoy if you organize your time well.

What would you do if only you had more time? Pretend you are working at a job and your boss says she will let you leave early if you can get all your work finished. I would be so motivated to maximize my time so that I could leave early! Then I could go outside for a walk, be with my children, or read a good book.

Now apply this idea to your own situation. Begin by thinking through a typical day. If every hour is full, then you probably are too busy, and this busyness may be causing you to experience defeat. As I mentioned earlier, examine your calendar to see where the pitfalls and the successes of your week lie. If Wednesday is your busiest day, then begin to think of ways to make it less busy. Perhaps you can eat dinner out as a family, find a carpool to help you with your afternoon driving, set aside a different day to visit a sick relative, and plan to do all your errands in one day. The point is to become aware of what the time-wasters are in your week and start getting rid of them. When you experience a sense of balance in your days, you will begin to feel more in control of your life, and you will be more motivated to continue working with, and not hating, time.

Actually, everything we do in life requires thought and planning. But because each of us is in a different season of life, we can't compare our schedules with anyone else's. I catch myself being drawn to the story about some woman who homeschools her twelve children while baking her own bread, running a new business, and saving the rain forest, and then I feel so inadequate! Please remember you have unique responsibilities and priorities that are different from those of other moms. Some of you just gave birth, and you can only do two or three things a day besides caring for your baby. Some of you are able to stay at home, so your energy level is higher than those who work outside the home and you have extra time that helps you stay on top of things. Some of you are working full time, raising children, and single, so there is no way you can do as much in a day as a stay-at-home mom. Don't become stressed because you can't do as much as you used to or as your neighbor does. If you don't have the time to make cookies from scratch, then don't! Use your time wisely by buying slice-and-bake cookie dough. I promise, your children will never know the difference. But they will know whether you are stressed out or peaceful. Do what you can to make a difference, and then don't worry about what you can't do. The big benefit of being organized with your time is the sense of peace and contentment you will experience.

*Procrastination is living your life with the brakes on.*

 ## *Plan of Action*

For our second step in becoming a more organized mom we have focused on ways you can "Manage Your Time." Where do you want to be in relation to the way you manage your time? How do you want to get there, with God's help? Look back at your response to Question #6 in the "Personal Inventory" section for this chapter. Do you still agree with what you wrote, and the order of importance you gave your three ideas? If you do, then complete the sentence below by writing in your #1 choice. Or, create a new #1 choice based on all that you've learned in this chapter.

With God's help I want to _____.

I think I will have to change _____ in order to make this happen. I'm ready to step out in faith with God and make this change, so I can begin to rule time instead of letting time rule me.

# Step 3
# Provide Healthy, Satisfying Food

**"She rises also while it is still night
and gives food to her household."
—Proverbs 31:15 (NASB)**

*I* don't know about you, but for me, knowing that "the dinner hour" will be arriving on the scene night after night is like watching a Hitchcock movie: my anxiety over its coming can be so paralyzing that I can't make anything at all! For me, cleaning the house, doing the laundry, running the kids around town, even changing diapers are nothing compared to preparing dinner. Planning and executing dinner every single night is my idea of a nightmare.

As I have spoken with and listened to other mothers over the years, I have learned that "dinner dread" is quite common. By the time most of us get around to starting dinner, we're too tired and too hungry to think straight. But whether we want to or not, someone has to be in charge of dinner—and that someone is usually mom. [Note: If your husband is the main chef in your house, then read this chapter together and discuss your "eating habits" and any changes you wish to make as a family.] In this chapter you will find plenty of ideas and tips on how to think about food, how to choose good foods, and how to keep the big picture in mind, which is to provide meals that teach good eating habits and create relaxed opportunities to grow together as a family.

You might be wondering how this step can help you become a more organized mom. I am a firm believer in the notion that if we first visualize a goal in our minds and then work toward the goal, we are more likely to succeed. If we want to become more organized, then we need to begin implementing ideas, tips, and steps in the major areas of our lives. As these steps become habits, we will become more organized. Nowhere is organization more important to the welfare of our children than in the area of planning and preparing healthy food. If we cut back on our busy lives and change our perspective on cooking, then we can turn this daily chore into something truly life-giving. I know these are big "ifs," but with God all things are possible!

Like most of you moms, I stay very busy. But one day I realized that my family was suffering because I never had time to cook dinner. My husband was missing home-cooked meals and my girls were missing the "family dinner time" that is so important for their sense of well-being. I began to look at my schedule and realized I was involved in too many things. I knew I had to stop some of my activities if I were going to be a mom who gives first to her family.

It was very difficult to wean myself from a busy lifestyle. But I realized that if I couldn't put a meal on the table on school nights, then I was just too busy. When I made changes, I experienced less stress and felt much happier, and the quality of our family life became so much better.

---

*Children who eat dinner with their families are 31% less likely as teens to use drugs, drink, or smoke.*

—National Center on Addiction and Substance Abuse

---

# Personal Inventory

Are you someone who prepares dinner on the fly, or do you sit down once a week to plan meals for the coming week? Do you often serve processed foods and order take-out, or do you cook mostly from scratch? Take a few moments to write down how you currently handle planning and preparing your family's food. Later in the chapter we'll look at what you might try in the future to become more organized and skilled in this area.

1. How often each week do you cook dinner for your family?

   1___2___3___4___5___6___7___8___9___10

   Never                3–4 nights                Always

2. When you provide snacks for your children, what do you give them?

   _____

   How often do you allow your children to snack each day?
   _____ x/day

3. What time do you and your family usually eat breakfast, lunch, and dinner?

   _____ The time varies every day.
   _____ a.m. (Breakfast) _____ p.m. (Lunch) _____ p.m. (Dinner)

4. When you pack lunches for your children, do you include a protein, a carbohydrate, a vegetable, and a fruit?

   _____ Yes                _____ No

   Do your children drink milk, juice, soda, or water with their lunch?

   _____

5. When you buy food, do you read the labels to see how much fat, sugar, and additives are in the ingredients?

_____ Yes                    _____ No

6. How often do your children drink soda or juice that contains high-fructose corn syrup?

_____ x/day                    _____ x/week

7. What are your children's Top 5 Favorite Foods?

#1 _____          #4 _____

#2 _____          #5 _____

#3 _____

8. In a typical week, how many nights are all of you around the dinner table, sharing what is going on in your lives?

_____ x/week

9. If you could change three things about your family's eating habits, what would they be? How would you number them in order of priority?

#____ _____

#____ _____

#____ _____

---

*Always have a fruit and/or a vegetable available at every meal, so your children get enough of these important food groups in their diet.*

---

 # Everybody Wins!

There are lots of great reasons for you or your husband to cook for your family on a regular basis. (For those of you who have older children, teach them to make dinner once a week, something they plan, you shop for, and they create.) Below are three benefits that, I hope, will motivate and encourage you to make changes in your family's eating habits:

- *Preparing meals for your family and eating together enhances the emotional well-being of everyone in the family.* Today food is available on almost any street corner, so if you don't cook for your older children, they probably won't starve. However, something else will go hungry: their souls. All children need to feel that they belong (this is the main reason teens join gangs), that they are accepted for who they are and not for what they do, and that they are competent in life. Your children learn these things first at home. When our children come home from school and we ask them about their day and cook a tasty meal for them, they feel loved and accepted.

- *Preparing meals and eating together teaches your children to make wise choices about caring for their bodies.* One day your children will leave home either for college or their own apartment. The years they have spent in your home will have been an experiment in the laboratory of life. Will they have learned what they need to know in order to make wise choices about the basic necessities of life? Are you teaching them now how to think carefully about the food they put into their bodies, how to prepare healthy food for themselves, and how to choose well when they are not at home? Your children will probably have children of their own one day, and seeing you give of your time in order to cook, teach, and lovingly steer them toward good choices is one of the best gifts you can give them. You may have heard the saying that the best sermon we can preach is the one people see in us. It's true!

☀ *Cooking and eating together helps us shine our light in a dark world.* Are missionaries who go off to distant lands to serve God the only people with a special call from God? Not at all! Each one of us has been placed where we are in order to serve God and bring glory to His name. "Bloom where you are planted" is the perfect maxim for the way God intends for us to live our lives. There have been many years in my life when I didn't want what was in my life. During those times I had to choose between being a light or a discouragement to others. I will always be one or the other—and you will too. When we cook, and invite others into our home, we become a quiet ray of hope that says "You matter." The Bible challenges us to "Share with God's people who are in need. Practice hospitality" (Romans 12:13). Around the world, friendships, relationships, and life itself are celebrated with food. These celebrations help cement the bonds between us. Moms, you can help preserve these traditions.

My goal in this chapter is to stress the important role family mealtime plays in the growth and development of our children's lives. These are the times each day when we can instill our beliefs and political views, teach basic manners, and share with one another all that's happening in our lives. Our children gain a sense of belonging, which is crucial to their growth and well-being. When we take the time to organize tasty, healthy meals for our family, everybody wins!

And if cooking is sometimes too time-consuming to fit into your workday, healthy take-out food is just fine! There are many places—Furr's, Luby's, Pickadely's, Boston Market—where you can buy good nutritious food. What is important is that you provide healthy food and a loving atmosphere where your family can be together.

# *What I've Learned*

Now that we know some of the reasons *why* we should cook for our families, how do we go about making meals without feeling overwhelmed? Well, this is a book about organization! The first step in preparing meals that make a difference is—you guessed it—to become organized. We need to lay out a plan that is easy, quick, and doable. Here's what I do . . .

*I consciously choose to plan, shop, and cook for my family.* Acknowledging a problem is the first step toward making a change in life. Once my older daughter left for college, leaving only Grace to cook for, it became easy just to eat out or put something together at the last minute. But when I did, this we missed out on the benefits that come from preparing a well-thought-out meal, not to mention the special feeling we share when eating food I make for her. So, I had to *choose* to plan the meals for the week and cook them, so that we would have more quality time together. Once I made this commitment, the process became much easier. Now I grocery shop on weekends, so that when I come home from work on Mondays, I am ready to make dinner. I can't begin to tell you what a difference this change has made in my confidence as a mother and the joy we experience sharing our evening meal together.

*I plan the days I will shop and cook.* Before doing this you will probably have to check with family members to see what their schedules will be for the coming week. If you have teenagers who seem to be away from home on most nights, then pick a "family night" when they *have* to be home for dinner. Your family will become much closer when you begin to eat and socialize together—without the TV! Statistics show that the single most important factor in keeping your children on your team, and safe from drugs and the illicit sex that is so prevalent in our society, is sharing family meals together. This is why I began adhering to a few guidelines:

- ❂ We made a commitment to sit down as a family at least once a week, and we said "No" to any meetings that conflicted with this time.

- ❂ I involved my children. I asked them to list their favorite foods, help cook, and set the table. I found that this was the perfect time to bring out the china and silver used only on special occasions, to show them that eating with the family is special.

- ❂ Sometimes, simple meals were fine. If I didn't have the time to make an elaborate meal, I occasionally served healthy take-out or frozen dinners. The important thing is to be together.

- ❂ I had everyone help with cleanup. I have found that one of the best ways to enhance a child's self-image is to give them chores and responsibilities around the house.

- ❂ We didn't answer the telephone or have the TV on during mealtime. You may even want to turn down the answering machine, turn off all cell phones, and tape that "can't miss" TV show.

- ❂ We did not rush. Since our lives were too hurried and busy as it was, we made this the one time of the day, or week, when we slowed down and listened to one another. We demonstrated love for one another by not interrupting when someone else was speaking.

*I refresh my mind on favorite recipes.* Pull out your family's ten to fifteen favorite recipes. These will be the ones you will look to each week for ideas of what to cook. When you grow tired of these, add new ones. Try to keep most of the ingredients from these favorite recipes in your pantry or freezer, so you can make a meal even when you haven't had time to go to the store.

*I decide what I will cook this week and make my grocery list.* Check the recipes and write down the ingredients you will need to purchase at the store. Cut out any coupons that apply to your grocery list. Walk through your house or apartment, to remind yourself of any other items you need to add to your grocery list, such as bathroom items, school supplies, birthday gifts, cards, etc. Try to shop only once or twice a week. This will save money, time, gas, and energy.

*I get my kitchen and workstations in order.* Look through your kitchen as if seeing it for the very first time. Open all the cabinets and step back so you can see what's inside. As you look over your kitchen, you will be able to spot trouble areas: too many plastic containers that are taking up too much space; too many out-of-season items just thrown into a cabinet; pantry a total mess with boxes of food dated from the 80s! Begin working from one side of the kitchen to the other until the drawers and cabinets are clean and up to date. Also, clean out your refrigerator once a week.

Then decide where your workstations will be. It's nice to have a station for making lunches, chopping vegetables, mixing and baking. Have the right bowls, knives, and cutting boards near these areas. I even have my sandwich bags in the drawer by my lunch-making station. Also, make sure you use different cutting boards and knives when cutting fresh meat and vegetables and thoroughly clean them after each use.

*I wash my hands before preparing food.* Make this a requirement for anyone who works in your kitchen. Leave out, at all times, a roll of paper towels (cleaner than a dish towel that is used repeatedly) and soap. Do not let your children get a snack after school until they have washed their hands. You can just imagine everything they have touched during the day! In fact, doctors repeatedly say that the best thing we can all do to keep from getting sick is simply to wash our hands.

*I set out the recipe, ingredients, measuring spoons and cups, pans, and bowls.* If you start to cook without preparation, it will take twice as long and the end product will not be as good. Take a few extra moments to set out everything you need, especially the dishes and pans. In the past, I would begin cooking only to find that I was out of an item! The rush to the store is very frustrating and time consuming. Also, the size of pan you use is extremely important. I keep a ruler by my baking dishes to make sure I'm using the right size pan. An 8 x 8 pan will make a difference if a recipe calls for one that is 9 x 12. Some recipes require a great deal of focus and concentration to follow. If the recipe is assembled or prepared according to different stages, go ahead and make one or two stages in advance. For instance, if vegetables need to be cut up or if some items need to be cooked together first, before adding them to the other ingredients, do this in advance. And remember to read the recipe all the way through to the end before you begin. You might complete the recipe, only to find out that it has to be refrigerated overnight before cooking!

*I start cooking and stay focused.* You've planned the meal, you've shopped for the items, you have everything set out in order, you've re-read the recipe, and your hands are clean: now the fun begins! Even for experienced cooks, it is easy to become distracted while cooking, and disasters can happen. Turn the TV off, keep phone calls to a minimum, and always keep an eye on anything cooking, especially items on high heat and oil heating in a skillet.

*Never leave the kitchen when these are on your stove.* The most frequent cause of fires in a home is unattended cooking. I have never left the kitchen with oil cooking, but just last week I got distracted cutting up vegetables, and when I put the garlic in the oil, it began burning. I was only two feet away, but the oil could have started a fire. So, always watch oil, time it, and keep the heat at medium to medium low. (If there is a fire, throw flour on it, not water.)

*I set the table, serve the meal, say the blessing, and enjoy!* When you have all your loved ones at home and around the table, all the hard work pays off. You are creating memories and showing how much you love them. I pray that as you adapt this method to suit you, cooking for yourself, your family, and others will become a simpler and more joyful time for all of you.

[Note: Wherever you can involve your children or husband in this process, DO IT! Their participation in this daily ritual will help them feel more a part of the family, and your children will learn skills that will benefit them as they develop into adulthood.]

 *Try This . . .*

Now that you know the basic steps in cooking, let's see how to make better, healthier eating choices. In other words, we've covered the *how* of preparing food, so now let's talk about *what* to prepare. Try some of the tips below to help you change from eating unhealthy food to eating better foods.

- *Respect your body.* Understand the importance of making wise food choices. Are you losing energy, your health, or your appearance? If your food is processed and contains too much fat, sugar, and artificial ingredients, it won't be nourishing to your body.

- *Make changes gradually.* Slow and steady changes are the ones that will last. Try slowly reducing the frequency and portions of foods you know aren't good for you.

- *Serve more water or diluted juice.* Rather than soft drinks or juice that isn't 100% juice, offer healthy choices to your children.

- *Keep junk food out of the house.* You and your family won't eat as much junk food if it isn't easily accessible.

- *Turn off the TV.* We tend to eat better foods, and only what we really need, when we are not distracted by the TV; and we talk more with one another! A Gallup poll found that, in the average American home, the television is on seven hours and forty minutes per day!

- *Choose the best ingredients.* The closer a fo ral form, the more it has to offer your fresh or frozen fruits and vegetables, Also, the darker, more richly colored fr generally offer the most vitamins.

❂ *Watch for long-term savings.* Eating healthy food reduces your medical bills, keeps you from having to buy larger clothes, and gives you more energy.

❂ *Read food labels.* Ingredients are listed on the label according to their percentage in the food. If sugar is the first or second ingredient listed on your cereal box label, change cereals; this means that sugar is the main ingredient you are consuming. If the first ingredient listed in your "wheat bread" is "bleached white flour," then it isn't *whole* wheat bread. Avoid sugar in all its different disguises (fructose, sucrose, and other "oses"). Stay away from juices with high fructose corn syrup, which is believed to be the leading cause of obesity in our country. Also, beware of refined fats. Anything that contains hydrogenated or partially hydrogenated oil will contain trans fat in similar proportion.

❂ *Beware of "fat-free" and "sugar-free" foods.* Sugar-free sodas don't have any beneficial ingredients in them, so it is better not to drink them. Ingredients substituted for fat can be worse for your body than fat itself! Eat naturally (butter instead of margarine, for example), but use less.

❂ *Resist all-you-can-eat restaurants.* A better choice is to eat at restaurants that specialize in quality and not quantity, restaurants that will cook food the way you want it prepared. If you want something broiled or baked instead of fried in butter, a good restaurant will be happy to do this for you, as well as make substitutions for you.

❂ *Keep a stash of healthy snacks on hand.* Get a cooler for your car, take groceries to your office, and keep your pantry stocked with healthy snacks. Know where you will be at mealtimes and what you will eat, so you won't be tempted to buy fast food or vending-machine food.

❂ *Teach your children!* Talk with your children about how marketing messages and gimmicks are designed to get them to beg for unhealthy food. Begin teaching them early in life about the way nutrition impacts their health, appearance, and happiness.

## *Tips for Moms of Picky Eaters*

✹ *Serve healthy foods.*

✹ *Offer a wide variety of healthy foods.*

✹ *Serve meals at the same time every day.*

✹ *Present food in an attractive fashion.*

✹ *Let your child decide to eat or not to eat—but if they don't eat, then DON'T allow them to snack.*

✹ *Keep trying! Your child WILL NOT starve, and eventually will eat.*

 # Set a Good Example

As with everything we do, moms, we are setting either a good or a bad example for our children. When preparing food, allowing our children to help us can turn this daily chore into a fun activity, and be a great time for learning. When you take your children to the grocery store, give them a list of items to get. They will be so excited to help you that they may forget to whine about being there or ask for everything they see. Explain to them why you are buying certain items and how you will use them; then let them help you prepare the food. When you are in the fresh produce section, teach them about the different fruits and vegetables. Do the same in the other areas of the store. Let them see how expensive some foods are compared to others, so they understand how important it is to organize a list and stay within a budget when shopping. Even if you have a toddler in the cart seat, talk to him or her about what you are doing. What a great teaching and learning opportunity this is!

Below are some of the best foods you can buy, organized according to categories. I am providing this list because I know how easy it is to get in a rut and just keep buying the same items. So, put on your helmets and get ready for a crash course in Nutrition!

*Fresh Fruits:* Berries, Cantaloupe, Mango, Watermelon, Plums, Pomegranates, Currants, Apples, Grapes, Cherries, Peaches, Oranges/Grapefruit/Lemons/Limes, Apricots, Papaya, and Frozen Fruit

*Star Vegetables:* Sweet Potatoes, Broccoli, Asparagus, Cabbage, Cauliflower, Lettuce (not Iceberg), Garlic, Zucchini, Kale, Squash, Onions, Tomatoes, Carrots, Spinach, Mushrooms

*Grains, Cereals, and Breads:* Wheat Grain Breads, Cereals, and Tortillas; Oat Bran; Multigrain Pancake and Waffle Mix; Whole Wheat Pasta and Crackers. [Note: For those of you on a low-carb diet, remember that your children need a variety of foods every day, including carbohydrates. Also, carbohydrates themselves do not cause weight gain, but refined sugars, the wrong kind of fats, and lack of exercise do put on the pounds.]

*Nuts, Seeds, and Oils:* Walnuts, Almonds, Peanuts, Pecans, Sunflower and Flax Seed; Canola and Soy Mayo; Canola, Soy, Olive, Peanut, and Sesame Oil; Peanut Butter; Hummus; Light Vinaigrette Dressings (Avoid Saturated Fats)

*Protein:* Fresh Fish & Shellfish, Canned Tuna, Cooked Sushi, Soy Protein, Veggie Hot Dogs & Burgers, Tofu, Beans (Lentils, Black, Kidney, Garbanzo, Pinto, Canellini, and Navy), Skinless Chicken, Chicken and Turkey Sausage, Pork or Beef Tenderloin, Lean Lunch Meats, 95% Ground Beef, Turkey Bacon, Eggs. [Note: Hot dogs are not on this list because they are one of the worst foods you can eat.]

*Dairy:* Skim & 1% Milk, Yogurt, Cheeses (natural, not processed), Low-fat Ice Cream, Butter. [Note: Dairy products are essential for healthy bones as well as weight maintenance. Make sure your children have enough calcium and water in their daily diet. One of the main problems with teen-agers drinking colas is that they aren't drinking enough milk and water.]

Moms, when you plan, shop, and cook as a family, you are teaching your children, by your good example, how to take good care of their bodies for the rest of their lives.

 ## Stress Busters!

As I have mentioned earlier, planning and cooking meals is sometimes a real hardship for me, especially when I am extra busy. So I appreciate anything that will relieve or reduce my level of stress over preparing meals. Here are a few stress busters that may help you:

- ☀ Choose one night a week to be "Pizza and a Movie Night." Order out pizzas, put out a dish of baby carrots and sliced cucumbers, and watch a family-friendly movie together. Yeah, Mom doesn't have to cook!

- ☀ Ask your husband or teenager to pick a night each week when they will be responsible for a tasty, nutritious meal. Help them with ideas, recipes, and nutritious advice, but don't hesitate to express your need for this help! Mom doesn't have to cook again!

- Eat out at a healthy restaurant on the family's busiest night. This could be the evening when you have to work late or your children have late activities.

- Cook one large meal on the weekend that can be divided into two for the week ahead, adding a fresh salad or different side dish each time.

- Use a crock-pot so you can come home to find your dinner already cooked.

 *Bringing It Home*

Of all the steps in this book, I feel that the step in this chapter is one of the most important. Why? Because when we don't put the proper fuel in our bodies, we just can't perform well at any level. For most of us, we will have to become organized in planning, shopping, and cooking in order to accomplish this. Most of us work outside the home, so we must put a system in place.

Here are this chapter's main points:

- In order to have food to cook and keep your children's stomachs satisfied, you must plan ahead. Plan your weekly meals according to your schedule, write out your grocery list, and allow yourself adequate time to prepare meals.

- Planning a family meal each day is as important for your children's emotional needs as it is for their physical needs. Remember, planning a family meal doesn't mean you have to cook every time. It's the planning and the priority you place on these that are important. There will always be days when you eat out together.

- Cooking healthy meals is not only a wonderful example to set for your children as you prepare them to leave home and take care of themselves, it also is an example of showing hospitality and Christian love.

Moms, I hope you have seen the benefits to yourself and your children when you become more organized and skilled in planning and executing meals. You will save money if you plan your meals for the week and buy only what you need. Providing healthy meals enables you to fill your family's emotional and physical tanks. Your children's general health, immunities, and quality of life will improve. You also will be creating lasting memories for your children as you prepare meals and celebrate birthdays, holidays, and special occasions.

One benefit bears special mention here. According to a recent United States Department of Agriculture statistic, more than 84% of children and adolescents eat too much fat; and more than 91% eat too much saturated fat. The source of much of this fat is junk food. Moms, we can stop this trend by buying and cooking healthy, nutritional foods, and by exercising more control over what and how much our children eat.

Another health problem we can avoid is the problem of childhood obesity and diabetes. According to the Center for Disease Control, between 1990 and 2000 instances of diagnosed diabetes increased 49%. Obesity is the root cause of diabetes and heart disease, and will soon be the number one cause of death in our country. In fact, when a child is obese, his or her quality of life can be compared to that of a cancer patient undergoing chemotherapy. Dr. David Ludwig, who has seen a growing number of obese children in his pediatric obesity clinic at Boston Children's Hospital, said, "Obesity is by far the single most serious medical problem facing children today." Moms, we must turn this problem around!

*A child's success rate is highest when the family is the most supportive and involved.*

—Psychologist T. Kristian van Almen

 *Plan of Action*

As we take this third step to becoming a more organized mom, we have discussed how to "Provide Healthy, Satisfying Food" for our families. We have covered a lot of ground, probably because food is such a huge part of life. We spend a great deal of time each week thinking about, planning, buying, preparing, and serving the food we eat. What issues or thoughts have come to your mind as you read through this chapter? What changes do you want to make in your family regarding your eating habits? How do you want to get there, with God's help?

Now look back at your response to Question #9 in the "Personal Inventory" section. Do you still agree with what you wrote, and the order of importance you gave your three ideas? If you do, then complete the sentence below by writing in your #1 choice. If not, create a new #1 choice based on all that you've learned and thought about in this chapter.

With God's help I want to _____.

I think I will have to change _____ in order to make this happen. I'm ready to step out in faith with God, pray for the wisdom I need, and make this change so that my family and I can eat well to live well.

Remember, mom, you are the parent and they are the children. You support and provide for your children by taking loving charge of the "what, when, and where" of eating, and then making every effort to ensure that the mealtimes themselves are fun, pleasant, relaxing experiences. When parents establish clear boundaries for when and what their children can eat, then there are far fewer battles at mealtimes, and far more victories won in children's bodies *and* souls.

# Step 4
## Spend T.I.M.E. Together

**"There is a time for everything, and a season
for every activity under heaven . . .
a time to build . . . a time to laugh . . .
and a time to dance . . . a time to embrace
. . . [and] a time to love."
—Ecclesiastes 3:1–8**

This is my favorite chapter in the book! I loved to be with my children and play with them in their worlds. In fact, for me the most enjoyable aspect of becoming a mother was re-entering childhood and living again the fantasies and fairy tales found in books, games, and theme parks. However, wanting to spend time with my children and actually doing it were two different things. This is where the importance of being organized comes into play. When my children were little, I realized that if I didn't plan my priorities and become self-motivated, then there would never be time to create the fun and relaxed home life we so desired. It was my failure to do all the things I wanted to do with my children that motivated me to seek out and adopt strategies to become organized. Once these began to fall into place, the transformation in my own joy and our home life was felt almost immediately, and my children and I began to love the time we spent with one another.

The key point in this chapter is that children spell *love* this way: T.I.M.E., especially when they are young. Mom, your children want to be with *you* more than anyone else in the world. Please don't take this for granted because, when your children begin middle school, you will end up on the "endangered species" list—and they don't mind leaving you there! Peers, music, and TV will claim the greatest impact on their attitudes, emotions, and activities.

Family time that is satisfying for everyone is one of the most treasured aspects of a good home life for both children and parents. Unfortunately for many of us, even those whose family bonds are close-knit, special times spent with our families are becoming fewer and farther between.

Social scientists suggest several factors that are taking a high toll on American family life: the conflicting needs and schedules of both parents working out of the home; the ongoing fragmentation of our civic, cultural, and religious institutions; the high rate of divorce and remarriage; and the enormous number of electronic distractions such as video games, computers, cell phones, and television. National time-diary surveys conducted in 1981 and 1997 by the Survey Research Center at the University of Michigan revealed that many families spend no time at all together. The statistics are disturbing:

- Overall, free time for children declined twelve hours per week and playtime decreased three hours per week.

- Household conversations dropped by 100%, which means that in 1997 the amount of time spent talking as a family was virtually ZERO per week.

- 58% of American families have the television on during mealtime.

- Structured sports doubled, from two hours and twenty minutes to five hours and seventeen minutes per week.

- Americans spend about 35% less time visiting with friends than we did 30 years ago.

While the average American family works 388 hours more per year than they did in 1969, the main threat to families is over-scheduling ourselves and our children. Most of us have at least some awareness that we need to spend time as a family, but we get caught up in the day-to-day busyness of life and forget to make this a top priority. A nationwide survey conducted by the National Youth Anti-Drug Media Campaign asked kids, "What's your anti-drug?" Their top anti-drug response was family and parents!

Moms, we need to make family time a top priority in our lives. We need to be supportive and stay involved in our children's day-to-day activities. And even though it appears they don't listen to us, they do: "Your child does listen and your influence will always be a factor," says clinical child psychologist Dr. Wade Horn, president of the National Fatherhood Initiative.

---

*Your family and your love must be cultivated like a garden. Time, effort, and imagination must be summoned constantly to keep it flourishing and growing.*

—Jim Rohn

---

 *Personal Inventory*

This section is one of the most important in the book, because you will get a sense of where you are in relation to the key component in becoming a more organized mom. We will look here at how much time and what sort of time you spend with your family. Are you spending a lot of time on the computer, at work, sleeping, exercising, watching television? Be honest. I hope this section will help you realize and evaluate where your time is being spent . . . as well as give you ideas of what you can do to organize your time better, so you will have more time to spend together as a family.

1. Right now, how much time do you and your husband spend with your children?

   _____/ hours each day (me)

   _____/ hours each day (my husband)

2. During a typical week, what activities do you and your children do together?

   _____   _____   _____

   _____   _____   _____

3. How often do you read to your children?

   _____ / minutes each day

4. Does your family set aside at least one time each week when everyone gathers together to share what is going on in one another's lives?

   _____ Yes          _____ No

   If yes, when do you do this? _____

5. When was the last time your family took a vacation together? What did you do?

   _____

   _____

6. Name three activities you want to do with your children that will help you grow closer to them? If you have more than one child, answer for each of your children. Then number the activities according to priority.

   #____  _____

   #____  _____

   #____  _____

*Children just don't fit into a "To Do" list very well. It takes time to be an effective parent when children are small. It takes time to introduce them to good books—it takes time to fly kites and play ball and put together jigsaw puzzles . . . These are the building blocks of esteem, held together with the mortar of love.*

—Dr. James Dobson, *The New Hide and Seek*

# Everybody Wins!

For me, I gained "family time" with my younger daughter, Grace, when I began planning and preparing our evening meal again. Earlier, as I became more organized with my time and had more time available for family, I began walking with both my daughters after dinner each night; this was a wonderful time for closeness and bonding with one another. Some of you working moms may be thinking, "That all sounds well and good, but I'm just too exhausted to do anything else!" I understand. But, try to write down at least one thing you could do with your children. If you don't, your children are the ones who will miss out and suffer, and I know you don't want that to happen. They just want T.I.M.E. with you!

# What I've Learned

In the long run, spending time with my daughters was absolutely priceless. When I said good-bye to my older daughter, Christi and she walked toward her college campus, I found myself wondering: Did I teach her enough and give her enough time with me during those few years I had her? I thought back to the way I handled some important times in our lives and how we were brought closer together because of them. I'd like to share with you some of what I learned along the way.

*The power of play.* One of my favorite ways my family spent time together when I was growing up was playing games. I did not know it then, but I was learning the whole time we played. I learned about counting, making change, and the value of money while playing Monopoly. I improved my spelling through playing Scrabble and sharpened my deductive reasoning skills while playing Clue. I developed the ability to focus, see patterns, and think strategically—all while having fun! I have passed these fun, beneficial times on to my children. Christi loves to play Monopoly, so one year for Christmas we gave her a Special Edition set, which now sits permanently on a table in the den, ready to play at a moment's notice! We also have Chinese checkers, chess, and Mancala set out, so we can play a quick game without a lot of effort. We spend more time together because, instead of turning on the TV, we stop and play a quick game.

What I like best about board games and card games is that you can begin family traditions with them. When Christi was about three years old, she received a game called Noah's Ark Concentration. I decided to pack this game for our annual trip to the beach. We both loved to play this game, and she began to excel at it. Now, every time we go to the beach, we have to take this game, and it brings back so many memories. The only problem is that neither Grace nor I can ever beat her!

*The great outdoors.* Another great way to spend time with your children is to be in the great outdoors. You can teach your children about camping, outdoor sports, bird watching, or gardening. Keep the activities fun and simple. (Don't make a garden or flower bed the size of a football field!) Let your children select the plants (appropriate to your region of the country), encourage their excited exploration, and enjoy watching the progress they make. My dad built a birdhouse for bluebirds. Once they nested, he would go out on the driveway and put down worms for them to eat. At first, they wouldn't eat until he went away, but eventually they began to tap the window with their beaks, letting him know it was time to eat! Now, whenever we go to visit him, we spend time together feeding the birds—it's such a great experience and a great way to be together.

*Reading together.* Even though I loved to be outdoors with my children, reading to them was my favorite way to spend time together. Reading is, I believe, the most important tool we can give our children in life; reading together was the one activity we did every day. I'm actually a "book-aholic," reading and buying books whenever I can! Over the years I collected books for my daughters, and now we have books for Easter and Christmas, picture and chapter books, and novels.

Every day after lunch, instead of telling my children they had to take a nap—NOW!—I would tell them to run upstairs and find the book they wanted me to read before their nap. Since they couldn't wait for me to rock and read to them, off they would go. And after bath time at night I would again tell them to go find the book or books they wanted me to read. But this reading time was different. I kept a stack of age-appropriate Bible devotional books in a small basket by the rocking chair or bed. First, we would read a "Bible book" and then we could read a "pretend" book. Then, right before I would lay them down for the night, we would call the other members of our family to come join us, so we could have our prayer time together.

After I read to the youngest child, I would then go to the older one. Sometimes I read to both of them at the same time, but my girls are five years apart and I needed to respect that age difference. If you have two or more children close in age, they might enjoy being all together.

*Exercise together.* Another way to spend time with your children is to exercise with them. After I had my first baby, I stopped going to the gym. Back then, daycare in gyms was almost nonexistent, and when it was available, it wasn't well maintained. Fortunately for me, I lived in the South, where the weather is warm much of the year. I began a routine of putting the baby in a stroller and walking, and this saved my life! Walking took away my cabin fever, built up muscles and endurance, and became one of the best one-on-one times I had with my children. To this day, I still love to walk with my girls. It's the best time for talking without any interruptions. Families that exercise together stay healthy together. Obesity is growing at an alarming rate in this country. We moms need to be the ones to turn off the TV, the computer, and the cell phone, and make time each day to exercise our children's bodies.

*Vacation together.* Some of my most vivid childhood memories are those of family vacations. I remember one summer when my parents took the family on a road trip from Georgia to California and back again in about three weeks. I was only ten years old, but I still remember the wild purple wallpaper in one of the Las Vegas hotels, the blazing sun in the Arizona desert, and my father stopping to help an elderly Indian gentleman who had wandered away from his nursing home. I remember the excitement we all felt when we saw the Pacific Ocean for the first time. I remember going to Disneyland (which was like visiting a dream) and visiting Hoover Dam, that great engineering feat. I remember gasping at God's creative artistry in the Grand Canyon.

Even though this trip was close to being perfect, we were still four children and two adults riding together in a car. In other words, things didn't go perfectly! My older sister got chewing gum stuck in my brother's hair, and while sitting in the backseat, they tried to cut it out without my father knowing it, so he wouldn't get mad! But what I remember most is that we had so much fun being together and seeing new sights. My mother was very organized, so we always had a cooler of drinks and sandwiches on hand. We would stop and have picnics along the way. (Back in those days, fast food hadn't been invented yet.) She also put plastic shoe racks behind the two front seats and filled them with all kinds of toys and games.

Later, as a wife and mother living in Colorado, I planned an outing one day a week during the summer months with four other families. We mothers would get together in May with our calendars and lists of all the places we wanted to go. Then we made a plan for each week. By the end of the summer our children had gone everywhere they wanted to go and done all the activities they wanted to do, but without begging every day! They could see on the calendar when we would get to go to their favorite places. We would plan outdoor activities like the water park, theme parks, Six Flags, and mini-golf, as well as indoor activities such as the Museum of Natural History, IMAX movies, etc. We would usually meet early in the afternoon and have a picnic first. My friend Sandy Welbon started this tradition, and it made our summers so much more fun and productive.

*Weathering crises together.* Some of you who are going through divorce—or just getting over one—may be feeling a pang or two of guilt about now, thinking, "How can I ever do enough for my children, now that I have even less time?" Let me encourage you to "Take heart!" When I was married, I didn't work outside the home, so I had more time to spend being and playing with my children. After my divorce this changed dramatically, because I was working. However, what I focused on was keeping our daily routines as consistent with the past as possible. We still had our family dinner each night. I still read to them each evening before bedtime. We still had snack time together, and we still had outings on the weekends. My energy wasn't the same, my time wasn't as plentiful, and I certainly didn't get as much done around the house as I did before, but staying organized according to our regular routine was a tremendous help in maintaining the fabric of our new family.

I also now had to organize time for my children to spend with their father. My children were older than in many instances of divorce; one was in college and the other was still at home. Still, I worked hard at encouraging the girls to contact their dad, spend time with him, communicate with him about the time of their activities, and pray for him. Do all you can to support your children's relationship with their father, because if the two of you can work together on behalf of your children, they will fare much better emotionally. And as time goes by, you will begin to heal and see the fruits of your labor to support your children, as they learn to adapt to the changes divorce brings into their lives. Remember: God uses all things (good and bad) to work together for good (Romans 8:28). As much as I hate what happened to my marriage, my family, my girls, and my life, our character has been molded more into the image of Christ as we have become people who are more mature, more compassionate, and less selfish.

 *Try This . . .*

The way you spend time with your children when they are toddlers will be very different from what you do as they grow into young adults. When my daughters were preschoolers they needed a great deal of one-on-one time with me: playing with puzzles, toys, and dolls; reading together; taking walks in the stroller; and just holding them. When they started middle school they wanted me to take them to the mall, to the movies, and out to lunch. Once they moved into the high school years they only wanted to spend time with me when they didn't have anyone else to be with, or when I would pay! It is in these later years that a mom needs to be attentive to adapting to her *children's* schedule. Sometimes teenagers will open up and want to talk as you are saying good night at the end of the day. Or it might happen when you're in the car, taking them somewhere. The important thing is that you be ready to listen whenever these small windows of opportunity open. They will love you for it.

Below are some tips that you might try with your preschooler, your grade-schooler, or your teenager. God bless you in your efforts to draw closer to your children!

- Take a nature walk and ask your child to gather "treasures" in a basket along the way. You can make a craft project with these treasures when back at home and discuss what the two of you saw.

- Ask your child to play an instrument while you both sing a song he or she knows. (For a toddler, banging a wooden spoon on a pot will do!)

- Limit TV viewing/computer use to no more than one to two hours per day, and do NOT allow either one to be on during mealtime. Make time to discuss with your teens what they are listening to and watching on the television and computer.

- Ask your children to help you set up a playroom just for them. You could all go to the discount store for colorful bins for toy storage and for small tables and chairs. Though this is a project for you, your children will get very excited helping plan their own space—and will learn great organizational skills too.

- Enter into your children's play area and just sit with your little ones, work on puzzles together, or read a book.

- When you first come home from work—if at all possible—sit on the floor and let your toddlers crawl all over you! Five minutes of undivided attention from you at this time will give you more time later for evening chores. And, your toddler will fuss less.

- Camp out in your backyard to teach your children basic outdoor skills. Make a campfire and cook marshmallows for S'mores.

- Set up a telescope (or go where there is one) and study the stars.

- Go to the library and choose new books, music, and videos to share together. For your grade-school children, make a special outing to the library to get their own library card!

- Give your child a camera to use, and help him or her create a scrapbook. Encourage your child to tell the family a story using the pictures he or she has taken.

- Build a birdfeeder or birdhouse together and plan feeding times.

- Organize a neighborhood clean-up day to give your neighborhood a facelift and be "other focused."

- Set aside one evening per week when the entire family shares a meal and talks about their week. Friday nights were always our "family nights." We would pick from a coffee can slips of paper with different games and activities written on them. But you could also have a predetermined topic to discuss. Expect your teenagers to respect this night too. They can at least eat with the family before they go out.

- Take each of your children on a "date" for special one-on-one time. Even if it's just to get ice cream, they will love the special attention.

- Pray both individually and as a family, not only when special needs arise but every day.

*Tips for Moms with Difficult Children:*

The tips listed above are just a few ideas you can implement with your children. However, some of you are going through tough times with your children, times when they are so difficult that neither you nor your child wants to spend time together. I remember one time, when my husband had gotten a new job, that within only a few weeks we sold the house, packed everything up, and moved from Colorado to Texas. During the move our younger daughter began really acting out. I would have to stop packing and repeatedly send her to the steps for a time out. Finally, in desperation I asked her what was the matter. Her response made me realize that our children need extra assurance, extra time, sensitivity, and love when they are going through major life changes.

Those of you who have difficult children, remember that God's power and love will *never* abandon you or your child. The parable of the Prodigal Son illustrates just how merciful and faithful our God is. Try to be intentional about spending additional time with your struggling child, and see if he or she doesn't begin to settle down, become more patient and cooperative, and show more respect to you and others in authority. Wise King Solomon wrote, "Reckless words pierce like a sword, but the tongue of the wise brings healing" (Proverbs 12:18). Moms, we are to encourage our children and make them feel wanted. I like to tell my daughters that "if all the girls in the world were lined up, I'd still pick you." I tell them this especially if they are going through a difficult time of testing. Children don't always like themselves, so having someone on their side can be the difference between floundering and making it in life.

*Tips for Moms with Teenagers:*

Spending time with your teenager is indeed a whole other subject! Unlike preschoolers, teens act as if they don't need you and can live very well without you. They try so hard to distance themselves, yet they really do want your protection, love, and security. Continue to have rules, such as family-night dinners, doing chores, etc., but begin giving them more freedom. Pick your battles: some things just aren't worth fighting over. When my daughters were in grade school, they kept their rooms picked up and their clothes put away. Once they got to high school, things changed. I still had rules about keeping their rooms clean and picked up, but it just didn't happen as often as I wanted. They wash their own clothes now, so if they don't mind that they're lying on the floor, they can't mind washing them again!

Let your teens become responsible. If they don't do a particular chore, such as cleaning the cat litter, then a privilege like using the phone, the car, or the computer might need to be taken away. Explain that if they talk disrespectfully to you, they can expect to have _____ (whatever is the most important thing in their life) taken away. Be sure to follow through with the consequences here, so that you teach them to make good choices. I promise, if you maintain your standards firmly and with love, they will understand you are in charge, not them. My mom used to say with great wisdom, "Remember who is the adult and who isn't!"

Since teens often don't want to hang out with their moms very much, it's important to involve yourself in their activities, attend sports events to cheer them on, or help with their youth group. Not all of these suggestions involve actually talking to or hanging out with your teenager. But your teens will be very aware that you are there—for them. Hopefully, they won't mind taking a walk with you, going out to lunch, visiting the makeup counter, or going to a sporting goods store. Soon enough they will want to start hanging out with you again.

*Tips for Planning Family Vacations:*

*Have a family meeting.* Children younger than five years old can offer a few ideas, but usually their main interest is eating an ice cream cone and running around. Children older than five are beginning to have opinions about what they like and don't like to do. Confer first with your spouse about the date, length of stay, budget, etc., and then ask your children how they would like to spend the family's vacation time. You might want to present a choice of three vacation ideas and let them choose from these. If children are part of the decision-making process, they will be more excited and better travelers.

*Research the travel route for places of interest.* When I was five, we drove from Atlanta to Ohio for my great-grandmother's ninety-fifth birthday. Along the way we stopped at Mammoth Cave and toured it. To this day I still remember that cave! By visiting the cave my parents turned a mundane trip into a vacation I still remember.

*Consider a camping trip.* Yes, you have to pack a lot of gear, but nothing can be as peaceful and free as a camping trip. Leave your cell phones at home or on silent, and be ready to enjoy the clean fresh air. If your children are involved in Scouting, they probably have some recipes for outdoor cooking. They might also be able to work on badges while camping. We camped as a family, and I also went to a summer camp that taught survival skills. I loved every minute of it.

*Plan a theme-park vacation.* These can be very expensive, but children love them. As a way of celebrating a special event such as a birthday, graduation, or Christmas, you might think about planning a family vacation to one of these parks. Contact different theme parks to see which ones will give you the best package. My girls simply adored Disney World in Orlando. So, I set up a large, clear jar and told them to start saving their money. Just before the trip we took the money to the bank, cashed it in, and bought the entrance tickets to the park. Besides learning how to save, they appreciated every second there.

*Vacation close to home.* If you have small children, it might be better not to attempt traveling long distances. Check with your city's parks and recreation department to see what events and programs are available in your area. If you live near a beach or a lake, see about getting a small cottage or hotel room for a few days.

*Vacation at home.* Even if travel, hotel, and food expenses aren't in your budget, you still need time away from work, school, and everyday activities. So pool all your money together and go to all the places in your town or city that you haven't had the time or money to do. Sit down with your spouse and set some ground rules first, so that it can really be a vacation.

- Check with your local chamber of commerce for tourist pamphlets that can give you ideas of places to visit in your area.
- Plan the places you want to go on your calendar.
- Eat on disposable plates for easy cleanup.
- Delegate the chores to everyone—because you're on vacation!
- Collect your mail—but don't open it.

- ❀ Let your answering machine pick up all calls, and tell friends and family you have gone on vacation.

- ❀ If you are unable to take off a full week from work, take one day a week, such as every Monday or Friday, and stretch out the list of places you want to go over the summer.

- ❀ Check the newspaper for activities that are free, such as art and music festivals and library activities.

Remember, moms, when planning your family vacation, resist the urge to overdo. Spending time with your husband and children making special memories doesn't require lots of money or exotic destinations. Keep it simple, have fun, and enjoy one another.

 ## Set a Good Example

As with anything we do for our children, one of our primary responsibilities is to set a good example for them. We want them to become loving spouses and parents with their own families one day. The question is, how do we prepare them? Remember, earlier in the chapter we discussed that children spell *love*, T.I.M.E. Let's look at ways we can model the importance of spending time together as a family.

- ❀ Decide with your husband that at night, when mom and dad see each other for the first time after a day at work, the first ten minutes will be theirs alone, to catch up with one another before being with the children.

- ❀ For you married moms, emphasize that you and your husband need special time together each day and a date night each week. I'm a firm believer in taking an overnight trip with your husband twice a year, even if it is just one night in a local hotel. Your husband needs to be first in your life.

In fact, the greatest gift you can give your children is to love your spouse. As you intentionally set aside time for your husband and then for each child, they will gain a concrete understanding of the importance of bonding in relationships.

☀ For single moms, your children need to see that you put them first, even before your dating life. And they need to see you take time to cultivate your own hobbies and interests, such as participating in a sport, being with friends, reading, or engaging in creative activities.

Children need our love, our attention, and our focused time. We have them for such a short time! And I promise you, moms, that when you do this on a consistent basis, you will form bonds with your children that will last a lifetime.

# Stress Busters!

Moms, we all have a great deal of stress in our lives. Adding even one more item to our "To Do" list can make us feel like we're drowning. So trying to come up with more time to spend with our family and children might seem impossible. Don't let yourself become overwhelmed here. Try to look at your situation from the viewpoint of eternity: what can you do that will have lasting value? Then, take a deep breath, refocus on the most important priorities, and try again. I promise that, even though the stress you are working under is heavy, "this too shall pass."

* The next time you find yourself about to lose your cool with your child, try making a really goofy face instead. Or laugh! Sometimes the absurdity of what I am upset about makes me laugh, which makes my child laugh too! I remember one time when Grace kept breaking dishes. Finally, when she broke a butter dish, I just said with a laugh, "If this keeps up, I'm going to have to buy a whole new kitchen!" It helped her not feel so bad. You'll find your kids are caught off guard by your playfulness, and they'll be more inclined to listen to your instruction if you inject a little levity.

* On rainy days, when the kids have "cabin fever" and everyone is whining or fighting, you too can become stressed. So, get out of that house and head to a museum, the library, a matinee, another mom's house, the mall, or go buy ice cream. Simply changing the scenery and having some fun will vaccinate your children against the deadly whine flu.

* If you have older children or a neighbor teen who can babysit, hire them to watch your younger ones so that you can take a break. You might want to just stay home and take a nap, go for a walk or run, or get some shopping done.

☀ Hire a younger child as a "mother's helper" to entertain your baby or toddler while you cook dinner.

Remember, if you take care of yourself, you can take better care of your family.

 *Bringing It Home*

Children know whether or not we want to be with them or whether we think they are "in the way." They know when our jobs, money, friends, and appointments are more important than they are. Mom, if your children do not occupy their rightful place of importance in your life, then it's time to adjust your priorities. Remember, all they want is for you to love them for who they are, not for what they do. Yes, you will always be proud of their accomplishments, their awards, and their victories, but let your children know that you are mostly proud of the person they are deep inside.

Moms, build strong bonds with your children that will keep them standing firm in God's truth and on your team, forever. Proverbs 22:6 says, "Train a child in the way he should go, and when he is old he will not turn from it." Training a child is a daily event.

One of the best gifts you can give your children is simply to be with and have fun with them. I know that for some of you, especially working and single moms, it isn't easy to think "play" when you have so much to do. I remember sometimes saying to my children, "I'll be there in just a minute," but that minute never came. So try to take time every day to be with your children, doing what they like to do, even if all you do is rock the baby, play on the floor with your toddler, have a tea party with your little girl, lie down with your twins as they drift off to sleep, throw a baseball with your t'ween son, or listen to your teenager talk about her life late at night. The stress of your day will fade away and the real joy of having your life and your family will come alive. Relax and play more—all of you will benefit!

Let's review what we have covered in this chapter:

❋ To our children, LOVE = TIME spent with them.

❋ Without the investment of your time, the bond between you and your children will suffer.

❋ Spending quality, joyful time with your children will help lessen the impact of day-to-day stress and any difficulties that might come your way in the future. Time spent in play today is like a vaccination against stress for the future.

 *Plan of Action*

For our fourth step in becoming a more organized mom we have focused on how important it is to "Spend T.I.M.E. Together." Have you gotten some new ideas about ways to nurture your relationships with your children? Do you know how you want to get there, with God's help? Look back at your response to Question #6 in the "Personal Inventory" section for this chapter. Do you still agree with what you wrote, and the order of importance you gave your three ideas? If you do, then complete the sentence below by writing in your #1 choice. Or, write a new #1 choice based on all you've learned in this chapter.

With God's help I want to _____.

I think I will have to change _____ in order to make this happen. I'm ready to step out in faith with God and make this change, so I can spend more time with my children and family.

# "To My Child"

*Just for this morning, I am going to step over the laundry,*
*and pick you up and take you to the park to play.*
*Just for this morning, I will leave the dishes in the sink,*
*and let you teach me how to put that puzzle of yours together.*
*Just for this afternoon, I will unplug the telephone and*
*keep the computer off, and sit with you in the backyard and blow bubbles.*
*Just for this afternoon, I will not yell once,*
*not even a tiny grumble when you scream and whine for the ice cream truck,*
*and I will buy you one if he comes by.*
*Just for this afternoon, I will let you help me bake cookies,*
*and I won't stand over you trying to fix them.*
*Just for this afternoon, I will take us to McDonald's*
*and buy us both a Happy Meal so you can have both toys.*
*Just for this evening, I will hold you in my arms and tell you a story*
*about how you were born and how much I love you.*
*Just for this evening, I will let you splash in the tub and not get angry.*
*Just for this evening, I will let you stay up late*
*while we sit on the porch and count all the stars.*
*Just for this evening, I will snuggle beside you for hours,*
*and miss my favorite TV shows.*
*Just for this evening when I run my fingers through your hair*
*as you pray, I will simply be grateful that God*
*has given me the greatest gift ever given.*
*I will think about the mothers and fathers who are*
*searching for their missing children,*
*the mothers and fathers who are*
*visiting their children's graves instead of their bedrooms,*
*the mothers and fathers who are in hospital rooms watching*
*their children suffer, and screaming inside that they can't handle it anymore.*
*And when I kiss you good night, I will hold you a little tighter,*
*a little longer. It is then that I will thank God for you, and ask*
*him for nothing, except one more day.*

— *Author Unknown*

# Step 5
## Teach Your Children Well

"These [ten] commandments that I give you
today are to be upon your hearts. Impress
them on your children. Talk about them
when you sit at home and when you walk
along the road, when you lie down and when
you get up."
—Deuteronomy 6:6–7

We parents are the most influential people in our children's lives. What we teach—both actively and passively—profoundly shapes their hearts and minds for the rest of their lives. (I say active and passive teaching because we are *always* teaching our children, consciously and unconsciously.) How intentional are you about what you teach your children? Do you think about what your child needs to know at different ages and stages of life? Do you talk about these issues with your husband and other leaders in your child's life, so that you are all working in a complementary way with one another? You need to!

Times have changed a lot since our own moms raised us, and things that used to be taken for granted and commonly believed— beliefs about God, showing respect for our elders, manners, taking responsibility for others—are now up for grabs. What's changed? Well, before the industrial revolution, most of our education and trade skills development were done at home. As communities developed into towns and cities, ways of learning developed into institutions of learning. Parents today have so many options when it comes to educating their children: public school, private school, home school, even online classrooms! "The basics," however, still need to be taught at home. Moms, we need to take seriously the responsibility we've been given to teach our children well.

You might be thinking, "But, Lane, I want to learn how to be a more *organized* mom. How can I get organized if I'm spending all my time teaching my children?" Well, dear friend, the more you teach your children, the more they will be able to do for themselves, and the more they accomplish, the more time you will have. The reward for your efforts is very real.

Our society has become so specialized. These days it seems there are "experts" for everything. Your children have school teachers, coaches, music teachers, Boy/Girl Scout leaders, daycare providers, and Sunday school teachers, to mention only a few. With all this expertise available, it's easy to "pass the buck" and let these adults teach your children. However, these people cannot teach your children what is most important. My daughters have had wonderful role models, but I am their only lifelong teacher.

In this chapter I focus on five skills and qualities that we parents need to teach our children: time management, home management, money management, personal care, and godly character. Please don't become overwhelmed at this point! These areas are meant to remind us what we should concentrate on as we prepare our children for adult life. Let me explain what I mean by these five skills and qualities, and then I'll share some ways I have tried to teach these to my daughters.

*Time Management.* We have already looked at how to organize time, so now let's focus on how to teach the principles of time management to our children. Until they understand how to work within the parameters of time, they will struggle to keep their heads above water. We don't want to turn our children into little soldiers, waiting for "0400" to do XYZ, but neither do we want them to be so lax that they don't live up to their full potential.

The important thing is to help them understand that time is a gift from God, and it is precious. If they waste time or forget to plan, they will miss out on all sorts of opportunities and blessings. We need to lovingly teach our kids to make the most of every opportunity God gives them. Let Jesus be your role model for keeping a balanced schedule. Jesus knew that spending time with His Father was the most important thing He could do. So first, let's teach our children to plan time to be with God every day.

One of the most valuable tools you can give your children is *how to tell time.* These days many children can only read digital clocks, which is like teaching your teenager only to drive a car with an automatic transmission, so they have no ability to drive a standard transmission if needed. Give your child a watch with a minute and a second hand as soon as he or she is old enough to take care of it, and ask what time it is throughout the day. Another important skill to teach your children is how to *read a calendar.* You might reward them by letting them add their plans to your family calendar. With the multiple activities that our kids have these days, they must also learn to *schedule their time.* As they watch you do this, and as you explain how it helps you maintain a balanced life, they will learn the value of planning their own time. When children plan their days and weeks, they are also learning about *setting priorities.* None of us can do everything, so we have to make smart choices. These are only a few of the basics of time management that we can teach our children, beginning at an early age.

*Household Management.* As your children become old enough to help you around the house, you can teach them the basic elements of managing the home. (Help is on the way!) My goal was that, by the time my girls went off to college, they would be able to take care of their own laundry, grocery shopping, meal preparation, house cleaning, bill paying, etc.

As early as two or three years old, your child can begin to do simple *chores around the house,* such as make the bed, put away toys, put dirty clothes in the hamper, and throw away trash. Take advantage of the fact that children love to help at this age, and make it fun to keep the house looking clean and welcoming. You'll also be building self-esteem when you give your children chores to do, because self-esteem comes from doing a job and seeing it turn out well. Older children can learn to load and unload the dishwasher, collect the trash and take it outside, take care of pets, collect and sort dirty clothes, and help with the cooking.

Little ones love to do *yard work.* Raking leaves into a pile (because then they can jump in it), pulling weeds (if you first show them the difference between the weeds and the flowers), and watering flowers are all things children will enjoy doing with you. Older kids can cut the grass. In colder climates your children can help you shovel snow from the driveway or sidewalk, and then make a snowman. Chores can be fun, and you can have a good time together if you help them view work this way.

A good way to teach *basic maintenance and repair* skills is by letting your children help you fix and repair broken items. One day your child will have his or her own place and will need to know what to do when a fuse blows, the dishwasher leaks, or the walls need to be painted. If you aren't very handy with tools, buy a basic "How To" book and encourage your child to take a class in shop or home economics at school.

If you show your kids *how to cook* quick, healthy, inexpensive meals, then they won't buy fast food as often. If you show them how to choose healthy foods now, they will eat that way when they become adults. Below are a few things your young chefs can do:

- Two-year-olds can use their large arm muscles to scrub produce, shuck corn, tear greens, and snap beans.
- Three-year-olds have good hand control, so they can mix batter, spread soft butter with a plastic knife, and knead dough.

- Five-year-olds have more refined hand and finger control, so they can crack eggs or operate manual equipment such as juicers and eggbeaters. Teach them how to use measuring cups. (This is also a great time to begin teaching simple adding and subtracting.)

- Six to ten year olds enjoy decorating a cake and making grilled cheese or PB&J sandwiches.

Children can do almost any kitchen task that does not require the use of dangerous equipment or sharp knives.

Before your teenager begins driver's education class, teach him or her how to perform basic *car maintenance and repairs,* such as how to pump gas, change the oil, fix a flat tire, and how to keep a car in good condition. Imagine and rehearse with them possible emergency situations and accidents, so they will know what to do; and always keep a first-aid kit in the trunk and a flashlight in the glove compartment.

*Money Management.* Teaching your children *the value of money* is crucial for their success in life. There are so many options today for how to spend, save, and earn money that they need your guidance, and early on! Begin by teaching your three to five year olds the basics of money: what each coin and dollar are worth. By age five your child can begin to understand the concepts of tithing, saving, and spending an allowance. There are even toy banks for young children that are divided into these three categories, to help them understand that money needs to be shared, saved, and enjoyed. Moms, you don't do your kids any favors by continuing to buy everything they need at this stage in their lives, because:

- One out of five teenagers in America does not understand that if you take out a loan, it must be paid back with interest.

- One out of four teens thinks that financial aid will pay for all college expenses.

- One out of three teens thinks that monthly Social Security payments will be all he or she needs to retire comfortably (survey from the Charles Schwab Foundation, 2004).

It has been said that the number one reason couples divorce these days is money problems. If we teach our children about the proper use and value of money, they will become more successful in their business *and* personal lives.

Help your children understand the value of money by (1) opening a savings account for your five to seven year olds, and a checking account when they are teenagers; (2) acquiring a debit card for your teenager, to begin teaching him or her that "plastic" is still money; (3) making a budget and sticking to it; and (4) saving money and making it grow.

*Personal Care.* Children need to be taught how to take care of themselves and, moms, usually this task falls mostly on our shoulders. If someone gave you a quarter for every time you reminded your children to wash their hands, brush their teeth, wear deodorant, eat healthy food, and take their medicine, you'd be a millionaire! Instead of giving you a laundry list of personal care items, I'll help you gauge how you're doing in this area when you take your "Personal Inventory" for this chapter. Then you can see where you might want to make some changes in what you teach your children about caring for themselves.

*Godly Character.* With today's "everything goes" philosophy, children have a hard time knowing what good manners look like, let alone godly character. You can begin teaching your children to "Do unto others" along with developing good manners as early as the toddler years. With these skills they will succeed in school, work, and their relationships. Plus, if you insist on good manners and appropriate behavior, you will have far fewer disciplinary issues in your home.

Small ways that instill godly character in your children:

- ❋ *Say "please," "thank you," and "you're welcome."* These are called the "magic words" because they fostered responses that were kind and polite; they are still the foundation of good manners. Today we see children grab when they want something, or even demand it. The root cause of bad manners is selfishness. We need to go back to the basics of politeness, patience, and doing for others first.

* *Write "Thank you" notes.* This is a common complaint from family members who take the time to send their nieces, nephews, and grandchildren presents, but never hear if they even received them.

* *Know how to RSVP for a party.* If children are not taught to respond right away to an invitation, it will come across as rude behavior, instead of gratitude.

* *Know telephone etiquette.* If a child is old enough to pick up a telephone and say "Hello," he or she is old enough to be polite to anyone who is calling. Begin teaching your children sentences they can use when answering the phone, such as, "My mom is busy right now; may I please take a message"? Also, cell phone use—and abuse—has become a tremendous problem in our society. Moms, teach your children not to talk on a cell phone when in enclosed public areas, because in a sense these hold those who are around them hostage to their call. Maintain at least ten feet of distance from anyone while talking on a cell phone. When shopping, banking, waiting in line, or conducting other business, don't make calls. If a call is incoming, teach your children to make the conversation brief and to the point.

* *Have a good grasp of basic table manners.* This instruction can begin when your children are young. My mom taught me how to put my napkin in my lap, hold a fork and knife, cut meat, and pass food politely. Children need to know not to speak when their mouth is full, and not to lick their fingers or pick their teeth. When they are ready to get up, they should ask to be excused and thank the host or hostess for dinner. They should also help clean up, since doing for others is a hallmark of good manners and Christian living.

- *Do not use foul language.* We hear foul language every-where in our culture. Although such language is common, God's Word instructs us not to "let any unwholesome talk come out of your mouths, but only what is helpful for building others up according to their needs, that it may benefit those who listen" (Ephesians 4:29). Establish stan-dards in your family as to which words are acceptable and which are unacceptable, and explain your reasons to your children. A good guideline to use is to ask yourself whether a word reflects honor and respect or the opposite.

- *Make proper introductions.* Nothing can help a new person feel more welcome at a party, the first day of school, or at any group event than when he or she is warmly introduced by someone else. Teach your child to be the one who goes up to another person and says, "Hi! I'm John." Children also need to be taught to introduce their friends to their parents.

- *Take turns speaking.* Teach your children that interrupting is actually a form of selfishness, because it says to another person, "I am more important than you and my words are more important than yours." Allowing someone to finish their thought shows respect and humility.

- *No "PDAs."* Your adolescents and teens need to be taught that PDAs, "Public Displays of Affection," are not appro-priate behavior. While it might seem cool to lock lips by their lockers at school, explain to them that in the long run this behavior will get them in trouble and hurt their reputation.

- *Choose appropriate attire.* This is one area where some of you moms may want to throw up your hands in defeat, or tar and feather me! The way kids dress these days is frightening! Girls don't seem to understand or respect that their tight jeans and tops, and uncovered stomachs, affect the boys and men who see them. Setting a different stan-dard is so difficult because it is hard even to find anything other than low-hung jeans and tight sweaters!

Recently, my pastor specifically admonished the parents of teens in our church to stand firm with regard to what our children should wear: "If it is too tight or shows too much skin, they can't wear it," was his advice, and I agree. If we are to represent Christ to the unbelieving world: "Do not conform any longer to the pattern of this world, but be transformed by the renewing of your mind. Then you will be able to test and approve what God's will is—his good, pleasing and perfect will" (Romans 12:2). Moms, I know it can be a daily battle, and I also know that we have to pick our battles when it comes to our teenagers. So, if they won't listen to you, then either take away a privilege or let them pay for their own clothes.

Moms, with all that we need to teach our children, nothing will be as important or life changing as teaching the value of things that can't be seen. Recognizing and affirming the qualities that make up a person's true character, the inner soul, determines who they are and what they will become. Stephen R. Covey, author of the bestseller *The 7 Habits of Highly Effective Families,* feels that, although it is out of vogue to speak in terms of character today, there is nothing more important in raising children. He wrote in *Reader's Digest,* Jan. 1999:

> *Character is made up of those principles and values that give your life direction, meaning and depth. These constitute your inner sense of what's right and wrong, based not on laws or rules of conduct but on who you are. They include such traits as integrity, honesty, courage, fairness and generosity—which arise from the hard choices we have to make in life. So "wrong" is simply doing wrong, and not just getting caught.*
>
> *Yes, some people wonder if our inner values matter anymore. After all, haven't many of our noted politicians and executives succeeded in every visible way, despite their moral transgressions? This question reflects a quandary of modern life. Many have come to believe that the only things we need for success are talent, energy and personality. But history has taught us that over the long haul, who we are is more important than who we appear to be.*

*Such eminent figures as Benjamin Franklin and Thomas Jefferson made clear their belief that we can only experience true success and happiness by making character the bedrock of our lives.*

However, as our nation has grown older, the foundation of our country, God's Word and His place in our courts, schools, and homes, has drastically changed. "In God We Trust" is no longer a standard belief, along with the truths of the Ten Commandments. As these beliefs continue to be pushed aside for the "rights of the people," the actions and thoughts that these principles stand for are also being pushed aside.

Since society no longer partners with parents as it did in the past, the best opportunity for your children to build character is within the family and home. This puts a great deal of responsibility on parents, but we are called to be an example as well as a teacher to our children. So begin first with yourself, modeling good behavior and character for your family. You can build and teach character at any age; it is never too early or too late to begin. The key is learning how to work inside-out and to rely on what God shows us in His Word. How can you do that?

- Test every decision you make with God's Word. Is what you are about to do consistent with what Jesus would do?

- Is your word trustworthy? Do you keep your promises?

- Do you readily admit mistakes? Do you ask your children for forgiveness when you have blown it?

- Are you loyal to your husband, boss, children, and other family members? Do you criticize them behind their backs, and then expect your children to trust what you say about them?

- Do you produce quality work? In other words, are you slothful with housework, your appearance, with tasks you need to do? Or are you consistent with "doing your best," doing more than expected, going above and beyond the call of duty. Do you show *and* teach your children how to go the extra mile?

❀ Do we work cooperatively with others? In a family we must work with an awareness of the needs of others. Are we teaching our children to be encouragers, good listeners, and good communicators, putting others first before themselves?

❀ Are we teaching our children, by our example, not to lie? When our children answer the phone, it is so easy to ask them to respond, "Mommy isn't here," when in fact you are! Changing that to "Mommy can't come to the phone right now" teaches respect and truth-telling. In fact, teaching our children the difference between truth and a lie is one of the main principles in character building.

❀ Put character-building words on your refrigerator and use them in your vocabulary. Use words such as honesty, loyalty, diligence, integrity, trust, dependable, courageous, cooperative, appreciative, servant, faithful, and lover of God.

Moms, you know how different each of your children is and how each one needs your help in different ways. One daughter wants you to teach her to tie her shoes; the other insists on figuring it out on her own. One son needs help focusing on his homework; the other has to be reminded to stop reading and turn off the light. Some four-year-olds remind their parents to pray and thank God for His blessings; others need to be taught to turn to God in all areas of their life. Work with your children's unique personalities, respect their differences, and begin at an early age. If your children are already teenagers, and are rebelling against your authority, don't give up on them! I have some suggestions for you, too, throughout the chapter.

*The best sermon ever preached is the one seen in us.*

# Personal Inventory

Moms, the reason it is so important for you to teach your children well is that they won't get the in-depth, consistent monitoring they need from anyone other than you. You are the one who has that "sixth sense" about them, "the eyes in the back of your head." You see their strengths and weaknesses, through the eyes of love. If we don't take the time and energy to guide them, they could get lost in the maze of life. As you answer these "Inventory" questions, ask the Holy Spirit to show you ways you can improve as your children's primary teacher.

1. Do you and your husband think of yourselves as the primary teachers of your children?

   _____ Yes        _____ No

   If not, who do you consider to be the primary teachers of your children?

   _____

2. Who else is "teaching" your children, and what are they teaching them?

   _____     _____

   _____     _____

   _____     _____

   _____     _____

3. What basic skills have you taught your children so far? Check all that apply. If you have more than one child, write their initial in the check box instead of a check.

I have taught my elementary-age child(ren) to:

- ❑ be self-sufficient on the toilet
- ❑ wash hands before eating and after using the toilet
- ❑ clear their place, help clean up, and throw away their trash
- ❑ hang up clothes, jackets, and backpacks
- ❑ brush and floss their teeth
- ❑ eat food when served, with proper manners
- ❑ keep their room, clothes, and toys picked up
- ❑ pray for God's help, thank Him for His blessings, pray the Lord's Prayer
- ❑ say "Please," "Thank you," "May I," "I'm sorry," "Excuse me"
- ❑ answer the telephone politely
- ❑ know their address and phone number
- ❑ know what to do in an emergency
- ❑ take care of their toys
- ❑ be a caring friend
- ❑ show respect to adults
- ❑ behave appropriately at church, in restaurants, etc.
- ❑ understand the value of money, save it, enjoy spending it
- ❑ give some of their allowance to church ministries
- ❑ read a clock
- ❑ perform their chores without reminders or complaint
- ❑ be kind to their siblings and do good to others
- ❑ do their best

I have taught my teenager(s) to:

- ❑ be a good steward of their (and others') money
- ❑ earn money and save it in their own bank account
- ❑ tithe and participate in our church's ministries
- ❑ obey curfew and rules with respect
- ❑ learn from their mistakes and failures
- ❑ set short-term and long-term goals
- ❑ grocery shop and cook nutritious meals
- ❑ wash their own clothes
- ❑ appreciate other cultures and races
- ❑ be caring and loyal to siblings
- ❑ treat adults with respect
- ❑ choose healthy snacks and foods
- ❑ say "No" to drugs, alcohol, cigarettes, and premarital sex
- ❑ drive safely in all kinds of weather
- ❑ keep a journal or diary

4. Name three ways you want to change how you are teaching your child(ren), with God's help. If you have more than one child, be sure to list at least one item for each child. Then number them in order of priority.

   #____ _____

   #____ _____

   #____ _____

*Treat everyone as if they have a sign around their neck that says, "Make me feel important."*

—David Holl, CEO, Mary Kay Cosmetics

# *Everybody Wins!*

When we teach our children the basics of being responsible adults, we equip them for a successful life. We build a foundation for them that will withstand anything life may throw at them. As a mom, we gain more understanding and control over who we are and where our place is, both in society and in the home. We are guiding our "gifts from God" to be the best they can be, and helping them find God's divine purpose for their lives. If we give our responsibility for teaching our children to the "experts," we forfeit that unique place God wants us to have in our children's hearts. You see, one day we will stand in front of our heavenly Father and give an account for what we did or did not do, with whom and what He gave us to work with.

# *What I've Learned*

My goal in teaching my girls was that, by the time they went off to college, they would be able to take care of themselves in almost every area of life. Here are some ways I taught them in the different categories covered in this chapter.

*Time Management.* Teaching a young child how to stay on task is hard! When Christi was beginning kindergarten, she was having a hard time with all that needed to be done to get ready each morning. I made a list of what to do first, second, etc. Once she had a plan, getting ready became much easier. When my daughters were teenagers, it was also hard to get them ready and out the door on time. I believe that teenagers should set their own alarm clocks and be responsible for getting ready on time. If they are late, then they have to suffer the consequences. I also gave

91

them daily planners and calendars, and helped them with planning their activities and goals.

*Household Management.* I have lived in many different houses and apartments, so I have had to learn how to paint, hang pictures, even repair plumbing. Growing up in a family of seven children, I was taught that doing chores is part of being in a family. Thank goodness my mom taught me to clean up the kitchen after dinner, because these kinds of chores became a fact of life that I passed on to my own children in our home. I taught my daughters how to take care of a house. My older daughter can cook and clean her own apartment, and my younger daughter can vacuum better than I can. But there have been some failures, too.

*Money Management.* When my girls were small, we gave them an allowance. I believe in giving allowances because the real world operates on the principal that, if you work, you will be paid. They each had a bank in their room where they saved their money for spending, for their savings account, and for their tithe. As they got older, they were taught about checking accounts and short-term/long-term savings. However, when one of my daughters was given a debit card along with a checking account, I assumed she understood how to subtract each debit purchase from her checking account balance. I realized after getting phone calls from the bank that she didn't . . . so we talked about it.

*Personal Care.* Having girls may have been easier for me than those of you moms who have boys, but I still had to teach them how to keep their hair clean, nails trimmed, bodies and clothes fresh, etc. Since many adolescents are embarrassed about their changing bodies and won't ask for help, I quietly bought them plenty of shampoo, deodorant, razors, etc. And I kept hugging them as their bodies grew into adulthood.

*Godly Character.* I feel blessed that I came from a godly family that stressed good manners. I believe teaching and molding a child's character is the most important part of my teaching as a mom. As a Christian, I believe in certain absolutes. I believe in the one true God and in His Son, Jesus Christ, so when I teach my daughters what God's Word says, we have a reason—God's truth—to follow that way. When my girls were children, they learned Bible verses, went to Sunday school and Awana, and learned about following Jesus. I don't believe in the idea of letting children decide who they will follow after they grow up; if I don't teach them now, the world will teach them.

One way of instilling godly character is creating awareness, concern, and care for others who are in need. I have always had a tug on my heart for children who live overseas in dire poverty. So when my daughters were little, we began to sponsor a child with World Vision, the largest Christian humanitarian organization in the world and one where more of the sponsorship money goes directly to the child than to other groups. This was just one way I tried to show my daughters how to give the gift of hope to another child. They are aware of the problems in the world and that we all need to look beyond ourselves and show compassion for others, helping them solve life-threatening problems.

 *Try This . . .*

Here are some more tips to teach your children about managing time, the house, their money, personal care, and character . . .

*Time Management:*

- ☀ Sit down with your children and help them structure their time each day. Help them set goals, budget time for homework/chores, plan a time for quiet, time for family, and time for friends. This is a great opportunity to teach your children about priorities.

- ☀ Institute a "No children after 9 p.m." rule. In other words, establish a set time after which you are not available to help with homework, sign papers, etc., and are free to have time with your husband, a friend, even yourself! Your children will see how you prioritize your time and will learn from you.

*Household Management:*

&#9737; Make a chart or list of the chores each child is responsible for doing. Create a reward system that is appropriate for the chore and the child's age.

&#9737; Because young children don't know what it means to "clean your room," take time to teach them how to pick up their clothes, straighten their room, and care for their toys.

&#9737; Set aside one morning or evening each week for everyone to complete their weekly chores.

*Money Management:*

&#9737; Let your elementary-age children work for items they want to buy; help them save, and then take them shopping! (It's the waiting and working for something—and the money that buys it—that bestows value.)

&#9737; When your child receives his allowance each week, teach him how to set aside a portion for church, some for the bank, and some to enjoy.

&#9737; Open a checking account with a debit card for your highschooler, and show her or him how to write checks, balance a checkbook, read a bank statement, and use an ATM, etc.

&#9737; Give your teen a sum of money each month so he can practice living on a budget. Give him enough money to buy shoes and clothes, entertainment, gas for the car, etc. At the end of each month, sit down with him and talk about his spending choices, the good and the not-so-good.

&#9737; Give your child an empty jar for her to put change in every night. (Any change lying around the house is fair game!) When the jar gets full, put the money in a savings account.

*Personal Care:*

- Have consistent schedules each day for baths, bedtime, eating, playing.

- At night, have your children lay out all clothing and anything needed for school the next day.

- Teach your children proper hygiene, the importance of health care, and that their bodies are the earthly temple of the Lord.

*Godly Character:*

- Read to your children devotional books, biographies of great men and women, and any book or article that will instill character traits you want them to have.

- When you fail or make a mistake with your children, ask their forgiveness.

- When you make a promise, keep it. This teaches your children that they can trust you.

- Teach them how to have a quiet time with the Lord, to read and study their Bible, to pray, etc.

- Volunteer your time. Just a few minutes can make a huge difference in a person's life. Five minutes is all it takes to send an e-mail to someone to encourage them, give hope, or just to say hello. Thirty minutes is all is takes to plant some extra seeds in your vegetable garden for a food pantry or to pick up some extra food at the grocery. In one hour you can read to children in your school, deliver food with groups like Meals-on-Wheels, or help an elderly neighbor balance her checkbook. You will be teaching your children that it really is more blessed to give than to receive.

*Tips for Handling Peer Pressure:*

- To prepare your teenager to deal with peer pressure, discuss the types of sticky situations they will face in the future. Role-playing can be useful here. Ask your kids questions like, "What would you say if your best friend offered you a cigarette?" or "How can you avoid getting into a car with someone who's been drinking?"

- ❀ Listen to your teens, even if you disagree with them. If you belittle their opinions or dismiss their problems, they'll stop talking to you. Instead, acknowledge their feelings and help them think through the different ways they might respond constructively.

- ❀ Help your kids discover their strengths and talents in order to develop a healthy self-image.

- ❀ Encourage your children to get involved in after-school activities where they can practice social skills and meet new friends who have similar goals and aspirations.

- ❀ Help them think through the cost that might come from making a right, but unpopular, choice.

- ❀ Talk with them about violence and pornography in movies, TV, and on the Internet, drawing attention to the way destructive messages about life and sex can be instilled through these media. My best advice is to monitor what they watch at your house and other houses; write and send letters voicing your concerns. An excellent resource is *www.onemillionmoms.com.*

 *Set a Good Example*

Moms, when your children see you keeping track of time, keeping up with a calendar, and organizing your priorities for each day, they will in turn follow your lead. When a child understands the concept of time, they can accomplish so much in life. As you begin to organize your home, room by room, and begin making

lists of chores for your children, they will live up to your expectations. When you talk to your children about how you earn, spend, and save money, they will think in those terms as well. As for personal care, I have seen moms who spent too much time and money on their personal care, and I have seen moms who didn't spend any amount of time on their appearance. Neither one is a good example for children. Above all, be courteous, respectful, and kind to your husband and friends, and it will teach your children how to treat others. Read your Bible in front of them and pray as a family, so they learn how to talk to God themselves.

 *Stress Busters!*

I know we have covered a lot of ground in this chapter. If you are feeling overwhelmed at this point over how much there is to teach your children, stop right now and release some of that stress. Maybe one of these suggestions will help.

&#9758; While it may sound too simple or too obvious, pray for your children and for your ability to "teach them in the way they should go." God promises that if we ask, He will give us the wisdom we need (James 1:5).

☀ One of my favorite stress busters is to lie down with my daughters to read or watch a DVD with them.

☀ If you have older children go to their room, sit on their bed, and just talk with them.

☀ Remember to laugh. Yes, you have a lot to teach your children, but look for ways to make it fun.

 *Bringing It Home*

Teaching your children the basic skills that will make them happy and productive as adults is what it means to be parents who rear children. In the book of Deuteronomy, Moses emphasizes that we are to impress God's commandments on our children. We are to talk about them when we sit at home and when we walk along the road, when we lie down and when we get up. In other words, we are to be teaching and instructing our children in the way they should go at all times and in all circumstances. Just take each day as it comes.

Below is a recap of the three main points in this chapter:

☀ You are the most influential person in your children's lives and their best teacher.

☀ Teaching our children is a 24/7/365 job.

☀ The best resource for parents is God's Word.

Moms, as you teach and your children learn, they will become easier to raise and more organized, and your home will become more organized as you find more joy in the process! We are not our children's servant. We are our children's teacher and encourager. And as they grow into adulthood, you will reap the benefits of seeing a mature, capable, and accomplished person.

One thing we have only touched on so far is teaching our children to learn from the hard knocks of life. Life isn't fair. Some children suffer because of their parents' mistakes. Some parents who work hard are cut down by accident or disease, leaving their children prematurely. Others who hardly work inherit the wealth of someone else's labor.

People of faith have just as many problems as people with no faith. King Solomon observed that life on earth fails the test of fairness: "I have seen something else under the sun: The race is not to the swift or the battle to the strong, nor does food come to the wise or wealth to the brilliant or favor to the learned; but time and chance happen to them all" (Ecclesiastes 9:11). For as long as possible we try to shield our children from the injustices of life. We talk to them about the benefits of hard work and good choices. We teach our little ones that good things happen to good people and that bad things happen to bad people. But we know that the rules we teach only work for some of the people some of the time in this life. If we seek God's wisdom, we come to understand, and to teach our children, that what appears to be a disaster really is part of God's perfect plan for us. God is shaping us, and our character, into the image of His Son. It doesn't seem fair to us, but our faith causes us to see things differently (Romans 8:28).

The following comments to high-school students lists eleven things they do not and will not learn in school.

> *Rule 1: Life is not fair—get used to it!*
>
> *Rule 2: The world won't care about your self-esteem. The world will expect you to accomplish something before you feel good about yourself.*
>
> *Rule 3: You will NOT make $60,000 a year right out of high school. You won't be a vice president with a car phone until you earn both.*
>
> *Rule 4: If you think your teacher is tough, wait till you get a boss.*

*Rule 5: Flipping burgers is not beneath your dignity. Your grandparents had a different word for burger flipping: they called it opportunity.*

*Rule 6: If you mess up, it's not your parents' fault, so don't whine about your mistakes; learn from them.*

*Rule 7: Before you were born, your parents weren't as boring as they are now. They got that way from paying your bills, cleaning your clothes, and listening to you talk about how cool you thought you were. So before you save the rain forest from the parasites of your parents' generation, try delousing the closet in your own room.*

*Rule 8: Your school may have done away with winners and losers, but life HAS NOT. In some schools failing grades have been abolished and they'll give you as many times to respond to a question as it takes for you to get the right answer. This doesn't bear the slightest resemblance to ANYTHING in real life.*

*Rule 9: Life is not divided into semesters. You don't get summers off and very few employers are interested in helping you FIND YOURSELF. Do that on your own time.*

*Rule 10: Television is NOT real life. In real life people actually have to leave the coffee shop and go to jobs.*

*Rule 11: Be nice to nerds. Chances are you'll end up working for one.*

— *Charles Sykes,* author of Dumbing Down Our Kids

Moms, read Psalm 73 with your older children. The author of this psalm felt his faith crumbling under the weight of unfair circumstances. But as he writes, he comes to understand that no one understands or anticipates God's final moves. Nothing had changed in his life, except his perspective:

*When my heart was grieved and my spirit embittered, I was senseless and ignorant; I was a brute beast before you. Yet I am always with you; you hold me by my right hand. You guide me with your counsel, and afterward you will take me into glory. Whom have I in heaven but you? And earth has nothing I desire besides you (vv. 21–25).*

# *Plan of Action*

For our fifth step to becoming a more organized mom we have focused on how to "Teach Your Children Well." We have focused on five areas where proper training is essential: time management, household management, money management, personal care, and character building. Where do you feel God leading you to train your child(ren) in new ways? How do you want to get there, with God's help? Now look back at your response to Question #4 in the "Personal Inventory" section for this chapter. Do you still agree with what you wrote and the order of importance you gave your three ideas? If you do, then complete the sentence below by writing in your #1 choice. Or, create a new #1 choice based on what you've learned in this chapter.

With God's help I want to _____.

I think I will have to change _____
in order to make this happen. I'm ready to step out in faith with God and make this change so that my children will be well-prepared to follow God where He leads them in their future.

*Refuse to do anything that your kids should do for themselves.*

# Step 6
## Discipline Your Children in Love

**"To discipline and reprimand a child produces wisdom, but a mother is disgraced by an undisciplined child . . . Discipline your children, and they will give you happiness and peace of mind."**
**—Proverbs 29:15, 17 (NLT)**

*I*n the last chapter we looked at the need for parents to be the primary teachers of our children. An important element in all good teaching is discipline. How does discipline relate to being organized? If we do not consistently discipline our children, then our own lives and our home life become unmanageable and disorganized. Good discipline brings order, peace, and balance to our lives. Below is part of a letter that was written to Focus on the Family, and published in their November 2003 newsletter, about how organization helped one mom:

> *I've heard Dr. Dobson say that your goal is to touch families—you've certainly touched mine! In 1978, I was a homeless single mom with two young children. I left the streets and entered the family of God. With no home and no discipline, my strong-willed little boy had become like a wild animal. Your books gave me direction, hope, help and strength. Now my 32-year-old son*

*tells everyone that, if I had not disciplined him and brought him up in the church, he would have ended up either in jail or dead. He loves and serves our Lord, and I have seven grandchildren who all know Jesus. God bless you!*

Moms, it is very hard to be consistent with discipline. We do this successfully by taking one day at a time, praying, and then praying some more. God will help you, bring you to the right resources, and bring others into your life to help. As a single mom, I have witnessed miracles in my life that came straight from God. I pray that this chapter will help you understand why and how to discipline, because as your children become better behaved, your life will become more organized and will be used to the glory of God.

It might seem contradictory, but we show love to our children when we discipline them. We set limits and boundaries to teach them how life works. Sooner or later, your child will come face-to-face with a teacher, police officer, Marine Corps drill sergeant, or an employer who expects orders to be carried out as specified. The child who has heard only "suggestions" about their behavior will not be prepared for the real world. It might be encouraging to remember that God disciplines too:

- ✺ "Do not reject the discipline of the LORD, or loathe His reproof, for whom the LORD loves He reproves, even as a father corrects the son in whom he delights." —Proverbs 3:11–12, NASB

- ✺ "Do not make light of the Lord's discipline, and do not lose heart when he rebukes you, because the Lord disciplines those he loves, and he punishes everyone he accepts as a son." —Hebrews 12:5–6

- ✺ "Endure hardship as discipline; God is treating you as sons. For what son is not disciplined by his father? If you are not disciplined (and everyone undergoes discipline), then you are illegitimate children and not true sons. Moreover, we have all had human fathers who disciplined us and we respected them for it. How much more should

we submit to the Father of our spirits and live! Our fathers disciplined us for a little while as they thought best; but God disciplines us for our good, that we may share in his holiness. No discipline seems pleasant at the time, but painful. Later on, however, it produces a harvest of righteousness and peace for those who have been trained by it."
—Hebrews 12:7–11

That last sentence from the book of Hebrews should be our reference point whenever we begin to struggle with disciplining our children. We want to encourage and so instruct our children that they will live a life of righteousness and peace. There will always be instances when we don't understand why our children misbehave, but we can understand a little of why they do what they do by looking at the way children learn behavior.

*Children learn through birth order.* In *The New Birth Order Book,* Dr. Kevin Leman says that children act in certain ways according to their placement in the family. Birth order greatly affects how your child perceives and understands reality. Whether a child is a perfectionist, achieving, cautious first-born (most of our astronauts have been first-borns); a mediating, independent middle-born; or a personable, manipulative, show-stealing youngest child, a child's birth order affects how he or she develops in the family, and later on in the world. Birth order explains tendencies—for there are never behavioral guarantees—that provide some insight into why children act the way they do.

*Children learn through taking power trips.* Of course our children need us, but they also want their own way. If your child learns to get your attention by throwing tantrums and crying, she has figured out how to get his own way through acquiring power over you. Tears, tantrums, shyness, anger, sulking, and pity parties are all designed to elicit attention, especially from adults in authority. That's why a "time out" is so productive. It isolates a child, removing him from the position of power and away from an audience. If you are at home, use a few minutes of time out for bad behavior. If you are away from home, simply ignore the "tantrum" child and walk away. Or, scoop her up and leave the situation without a fuss. Don't follow the temptation to give in or argue back. Once your little one sees you are not giving in to the manipulative behavior, she or he will learn that this behavior doesn't work. (Teenagers need to be dealt with somewhat differently, but we'll discuss them later in this chapter.) Remember, each child has a different temperament and different needs and issues.

*Children learn by watching their parents.* We can talk to our children until we are blue in the face, but what they *see* us do is worth a thousand words. Your children begin life believing you and your husband are the most important people in the world. As they grow, teachers and other family members begin to exert influence over them. When children become teens, friends become a tremendous influence in one another's lives, which is why we need to give loving, consistent discipline beginning very early in life. We need to model honesty, open up avenues for discussion, and strengthen our relationships with them. When you admit your mistakes and ask for your child's forgiveness, then you also teach your children to apologize and ask for forgiveness from others when they make a mistake. They need to see and understand that no one is perfect.

*Children learn through their own temperaments.* There are countless books that can help you recognize and understand the different temperaments people have. I recommend Florence Littauer's *Personality Plus.* Understanding your child's temperament can be a tremendous help in understanding how to discipline a child. Moms, no matter what your child is like, she or he still needs ground rules, training, and discipline.

There are three types of parents, but only one that works. An *authoritarian* parent says, "You will do what I tell you to do no matter what!" Authoritarian parents believe their way is the only way. The problem is that eventually children want to assert their own ideas and eventually they may rebel against this type of parental authority. A *permissive* parent is one who really wants her children to like her and be her friend. Don't try to be your children's friend! They have plenty of friends, but only one mom! They need you to be their parent. You can be their friend when they turn twenty-one. Permissiveness actually fosters rebellion, for children become angry when they are not given boundaries and rules that create order and structure. An *authoritative* parent understands her position in the family, and is mature enough to engage in conversation with her children because they value her ideas. Authoritative parents establish relationships with their children based on trust, loyalty, kindness, and respect. Their children understand that if they do wrong, there will be consequences, but they also know that these will be fair. The parent has the last say but is always willing to listen to the child. God wants us to be authoritative moms.

### Reasons Children Misbehave

- ☀ *to gain attention*
- ☀ *to acquire power and get what they want*
- ☀ *to get revenge*
- ☀ *they have medical and emotional problems*
- ☀ *they aren't being understood*

 ## Personal Inventory

Before I present suggestions and personal stories—including some reflections from "experts" in child psychology—I want to give you time to think about where you are with the whole subject of disciplining your children. Give this section careful thought, because when you see where you really are, then where you want to be and how you will get there become clearer and easier. Take a few moments to answer the following questions about your current thoughts and habits regarding discipline.

1. What kind of parenting style do you have: authoritarian, permissive, or authoritative? You may want to review the definitions of these three styles in the previous section before you answer. Explain your choice.

   _____

   _____

2. Explain how you decide what type of discipline is appropriate for a given misbehavior.

   _____

   _____

3. Describe the difference between discipline and punishment.

   _____

   _____

4. What are some ways that you punish rather than discipline your children?

   _____

   _____

5. Name three areas where you want to begin disciplining your children differently. If you have more than one child, think of at least one idea for each child. Then number your answers according to priority.

   #____ _____

   #____ _____

   #____ _____

*Do not tell your children they are "bad."*
*Focus on the bad behavior and work together to change it.*

# *Everybody Wins!*

When we discipline consistently and correctly, everybody in the family—and even in society—wins. You see, moms, as much as you want to baby your children and make life easier for them, if you don't discipline them, they will begin to feel that you don't love them. Our human nature *needs* boundaries and guidelines, or we spin out of control. That's why parenting is such a hands-on, 24/7/365 occupation. For children to develop emotionally, socially, mentally, and spiritually, they need strong but loving parents to guide them.

Moms, if your home and personal life are not organized, then you won't have time, energy, or the ability to properly discipline your children. And the reality is that you won't be able to see how much of a problem is developing within them until later on, when the problem becomes *really* hard to handle. Another problem with not being organized enough to discipline is that you will miss out on the bonding that is part of the process of good discipline.

It's never too late to begin good disciplinary habits! Begin disciplining your children right now. When you set consistent, thoughtful boundaries, you will begin to see positive changes in your children's behavior and sense of well being.

# *What I've Learned*

One thing I have learned is that children are looking for us to fulfill particular, basic human needs—what I call the ABCs. When we diligently use the ABC approach, our children flourish and there is more harmony in the home. If you can remember "ABC," then you can remember the following tips.

First, children look to us for unconditional ACCEPTANCE of who they are as individuals. As I have mentioned before, every child is different. However, if your child doesn't feel that you accept her (he isn't the same size as his brother, she doesn't make good grades like her sister, he prefers music to sports, she has a physical problem, he is forgetful, etc.), her self-esteem and her heart drop. Children *must* feel accepted and loved unconditionally in the only place that is truly God-given to them—the family. Moms, this can be hard to do when your adolescent seems to stumble and trip all the time, smell badly, or just act obnoxious! But please don't show favoritism among your children. When Rachel and Isaac allowed their favoritism to get the best of them, there was great trouble for Jacob and Esau.

Since my daughters are five years apart, it was easier for me to treat each one as special. However, as they became more involved in activities, my younger daughter thought she had to do everything her big sister had done. Reassure your children that they don't have to compete with *anyone,* especially a sibling.

Second, children look to us for a sure and unmistakable sense of BELONGING. Do you know the main reason gangs are so popular? It's because, for so many teens, this is the one place where they experience a sense of belonging. Children have a desperate need to feel they belong, and if they don't feel this sense of belonging in the family, then they will do anything to become part of a group, even if that group has a destructive effect on them. This is why encouraging your children to join different clubs at school or church is so beneficial. Also, be sensitive to your children if they have to move to a new school. The desperate need to have friends and be part of a group can easily cause children and teens to begin hanging out with the wrong crowd. Remember that most kids don't set out to be "bad" kids. They simply have a basic need to belong to a group, and if they can't find the right group, they will take up with whatever else becomes available to them.

Moms, remember that popularity isn't the only thing that matters. I'd rather my girls have one or two lifelong friends than be the most popular girls in school. Why? Experiencing close relationships is an essential part of having a healthy sense of belonging. In close friendships children experience a sense of contributing something in return for what is given to them, and this makes them feel good about themselves. My mom always encouraged us not only to have friends but to have them come to our home. I was always allowed to host spend-the-night parties and other get-togethers with friends. My mom became involved with my friends and knew the names of every friend all seven of us had! So, I have tried to do all I can to love and welcome my girls' friends.

Third, children look to us—they *trust* us—to help them develop the COMPETENCE they need in order to take care of themselves and handle the responsibilities and challenges that come their way in life. You may have come across the saying that goes, "No one can do everything, but everyone can do something." Build your children's sense of competence by focusing on what they *can* do, not on what they can't do. What they can do is usually revealed in their hobbies and interests. My sister Carol has a precious daughter who loves and understands animals. Although it takes time, money, and effort on Carol's part, she consistently supports Carly's interests. They now have two dogs, one cat, one bird (that flies around the house and sits on everyone's shoulders!), one lizard, and a few mice! Remember, it is so important that you allow your children the freedom to be different from you. Be extremely careful not to be critical in assessing your child's abilities and interests. Children can become so utterly discouraged by just one critical remark from you. But the good results they achieve through participating and working with something that interests them, and learning to make decisions on their own, are extremely important in developing a healthy sense of self-esteem and success in life.

 *Try This . . .*

For some of you moms, the previous section may sound too easy. When your two-year-old continues to display temper tantrums or your teenager "freezes you out" with his or her body language and sharp tongue, it's hard to imagine that things can or will ever change. I promise they will. What can you do to get your child to behave? Try some of these tips . . .

- Be an authoritative, not authoritarian, parent.

- Make a list of what you expect from your children and the consequences of not meeting those expectations.

- Make a contract with your teenager, spelling out how you want him or her to participate in your family's life and the consequences if either one of you breaks the contract. Both of you sign the contract. That way you become accountable to one another.

- Discuss and write down the consequences of unacceptable behavior before it happens. And be consistent! Children need to know what to expect.

- Allow your children to experience the consequences of their misbehavior. Teach them how to repent, apologize, and be responsible for their actions.

- Don't discipline your children in anger, but do take swift action.

- Tailor discipline according to the offense.

- Remind your child that you love him or her, but not the behavior. After imposing discipline, bring closure to the event by discussing your reason for the discipline; then have your child ask for forgiveness and a hug!

Good discipline hits children where they are and where it "hurts." Remember, moms, our job is to train and encourage our children to develop behavior patterns that enable them to be successful and respected in life.

Parents are given the daunting task of raising up the next generation of adults. But there can be a fine line between meeting our responsibilities as parents and the way our children turn out. Children, as they mature, have the power and right to make their own choices, for good or for bad. We can't go through life feeling guilty for the things we did or didn't do, or should or shouldn't have done. Yet, we need to strive to be the best moms we can be with the light we are given at each moment. That is why I highly suggest praying each day for God to give you wisdom in raising your children. I also suggest gathering resources, teachers, and counselors to work with you whenever you find yourself in a difficult place.

No child is perfect and no parent is perfect! Remember, God's first children, Adam and Eve, disobeyed Him, and the sibling rivalry and felt hatred between his first grandchildren were bitter and destructive. But just as God continued to love His children and show them the way, so we are to do the same for our children.

This leads us to examine our lives and the way we relate to our children. We need to ask whether or not we are being loving, caring, and intelligent parents. Children model what they see us do. We need to be conscious and diligent in how we live our lives and the choices we make. Here are some additional tips on how to relate to your children that will help you mold, train, and discipline them:

*Model the Golden Rule.* The foundation for creating strong relationships is to treat others as we want others to treat us (Matthew 7:12). The way you engage with your friends, relatives, and associates should be repeated with your children. We need to show respect, loyalty, truthfulness, forgiveness, encouragement, acceptance, and concern for their welfare; and to protect them from harm.

*Listen to your children.* If we listen actively to our children, they will want to be on our side. "Everyone should be quick to listen, slow to speak and slow to become angry" (James 1:19). As you listen to your children, summarize back to them what you hear them saying. When they feel they are really being heard, they will trust and share with you more. Do not lecture, threaten, or offer immediate correction when your children are talking to you. This is the time to look into their eyes and even lean your body toward them: focus on them.

*Control your anger.* Although we all experience irritation, frustration, and anger with our children, we need to direct our feelings at the behavior rather than our child. Yes, this is very difficult to do, but I found that if I kept my voice very low and quiet and responded with a question like, "What should we do about your talking back?" there was a better chance of keeping a connection with my child and resolving the issue, rather than having her storm back to her room.

*Comfort and encourage your children.* When children are disappointed and discouraged, listen to them, empathize with them, and respond to their feelings. Do not tell them "it doesn't matter," "just shake it off," or "be tough." Don't let them control you with their problems and don't allow unacceptable behavior, but do empathize and sympathize with their hurts and disappointments.

*Don't nag.* If you make it a house rule that something is asked only once and then there are consequences for not responding, then you won't have to nag! For instance, tell your children that in ten minutes it will be time to go do errands. If, after ten minutes you call everyone to the car and no one comes, then simply remind them that if you have to repeat yourself, then the car for errands will no longer be working for whatever they want to do later. Then be sure to follow through, mom! When they later ask to be driven to the pool, calmly remind them that the consequence of not responding to your request was no trip to the pool. I promise: if you are consistent, your children will suddenly develop great listening and response skills.

*Love your children.* Nothing is as important as loving your children. Tell them you love them every day, but also *show* them you love them. Love is not about giving things; it's about giving of yourself, your time, and your energy. Children can spot the real thing. They need to know you are interested in them personally and that you want the best for them. Building solid relationships with your children is the key to being a great authority figure.

*The Teenage Years . . .*

There comes a time—the teenage years—when many of us parents feel that we have lost control of our child and have failed as a parent. I know that the words *relationship, teenager,* and *survive* don't typically appear in the same sentence, but it really is possible to grow close to your teenager. I feel closer to my twenty-two-year-old and seventeen-year-old daughters now than when they were babies. We share a sense of closeness and bonding now that makes all the hardships of the earlier years worthwhile. We go shopping, out to lunch, and play tennis, and I can relax and enjoy these wonderful people they have become.

Building relationship is the first step in disciplining teenagers. Hopefully, you have begun showing understanding, compassion, respect, and a willingness to listen before your children get to this stage. Now that they are growing up, we have to adapt our methods, especially in giving them more freedom. Here are some tips on ways you can not only survive but *thrive* during the teen years:

- ◉ Create a home where your teenager and friends want to hang out.
- ◉ Pick your battles carefully, and then be firm and consistent.
- ◉ Let them make mistakes and experience the consequences.
- ◉ Expect the best from them.
- ◉ Be available to listen.
- ◉ Moodiness is normal at this age, so try not to overreact.

- Respect your teen's privacy.

- Role-play potential problem situations involving the offer of cigarettes, drugs, alcohol, and sex.

- NEVER embarrass your teen!

- Show that you trust them by giving them responsibilities.

- Pray for your children's choices regarding their future, school, job, and spouse.

Moms, this transition time is hard on everyone. I know, I've been there, done that, and bought the T-shirt! But your teenagers really are growing into wonderful, new people. Enjoy the process!

*When Things Don't Go as Planned . . .*

Some of you reading this chapter may feel like you are at a dead end. You are way past the tips mentioned above; your child has already rebelled against you and gotten into drugs or alcohol, or has maybe even run away, dropped out of school, or is living with someone else. He or she has completely rejected your values, your morals, and your God. Not only are you suffering heartbreak over the change in your child and the loss of who he or she was, but you also feel the embarrassment and judgment of others.

Mom, there is a Bible story that was written just for your situation and your pain. Read the story of the Prodigal Son in Luke 15. When the younger son went to his father for his inheritance, he didn't ask for it, he demanded it! In doing so he implied that his father was as good as dead to him, because normally his inheritance would only come upon his father's death. So, here we have a rebellious son who is running away from home, rejecting all the love, teaching, memories, and traditions his father gave him. Yet the father wisely gives his son what he demands. (I think I would have grabbed an ear and given a very long grounding!) In giving his son what he asks for he shows us that there really does comes a time when we have done all we can do, and our child must be set free to make his or her own decisions, good or bad. You know the rest of the story: the son "comes to his senses," repents, and comes back home with a humbled heart and a changed attitude. My dear mom, this is what I pray will happen with your child and your family.

If you cannot change the situation, then what *can* you do when your child rebels? First, don't ignore your pain. Go to God and cry out to Him about the hurt and pain you are feeling. God promises never to leave you. He will be your Rock and your Comfort. And be gentle with yourself—no parent is perfect—but take time to review the past, humble yourself before God, and repent of those things you did or did not do. Then let God take this burden from you. Apart from Christ, we can do nothing. We have a God who can do miracles. Stand firm in your faith so that when your child comes back, he or she will see your trust in the Lord. Be ready to run to your child at that point! (When the prodigal son returned, his father ran to him, which was considered an inappropriate action in those days.) While you wait expectantly, get some outside help, either from a family counselor, your pastor, or the youth pastor of your church. Find a support group in your church or community where you can be with others who are going through the pain you are. And please know that many church leaders have known the pain of coping with rebellious children, so don't judge yourself.

If you are having a hard time knowing what to do or how to parent your child, I hope the comments and stories provided in the next section will help you feel that you are not alone, and give you hope for your child and your family.

# Set a Good Example

Setting a good example for our children and others is difficult, especially if you make mistakes in the very area where you are supposed to be an expert! I want to share with you some reflections written by child-care professionals about the mistakes they made raising their own children (excerpted from Bonnie Miller Rubin's article, "Parenting Experts Confess," *Good Housekeeping* [June 2004]:

119). As you read about the way these parents raised their children and realized they were making mistakes, I hope you'll get a great big dose of hope and some ideas that might help your own situation.

*Sally Shaywitz, M.D., is a neuroscientist and author in New Haven, Connecticut. She is also the mother of three sons, twins who are thirty-four and another who is thirty-six. Dr. Shaywitz writes that, "When my children were growing up, I was a very young and inexperienced mother. I believed everything had to be perfect. It seemed to matter so much that they were each in the right classes, did well in school, participated in sports activities, and took music lessons. Today, with the advantage of hindsight, I would be so much more laid-back and relaxed. I certainly would have more faith in my children's innate strengths. I would let them follow their instincts rather than make presumptive decisions about what I thought was best for them. And I would appreciate that it's OK, perhaps even preferable, for children to do nothing and to spend time imagining than to constantly be scheduled up with activities."*

*Mary Pipher, Ph.D., is a psychologist and author in Lincoln, Nebraska, who is also the mother of a twenty-seven-year-old daughter and a son who is thirty-three. If she could, she would have done things differently: "When I was young, my mother was in medical school and my father was in the military. They were just like God to me but not as available as I would have liked. So one of my goals with my own kids was to just be nurturing, to protect them from the knocks. But I think I erred in the direction of trying a little too hard to make sure that they didn't suffer. If they were irresponsible and left something out in the rain, I was more than happy to help them replace it. I made sure that whatever mistakes they made didn't cost them too dearly. But when we're adults, we see that our actions have consequences. So I'd cushion less and let them feel the full weight of their consequences more."*

*William Damon, Ph.D., is a professor of education and an author in Stanford, California, and the father of two daughters, ages twenty and twenty-seven, and a son who is thirty. Dr. Damon writes that "I would have shared some of the burdens a little more by the time my kids were 12 or so. There were times when my wife and I were stressed out about something—work or finances. Rather than talk about our worries in front of the kids, we'd shelter them. So all they saw was the anxiety. Kids are smart, and ours knew their parents were worried. And they knew we solved the problems, but they didn't know how. There are some conflicts—such as marital—that you don't bring the kids into, but there's no need to completely shield them from everything. It strengthens kids to confront real life, especially if they confront it with your guidance."*

I hope these true stories from "experts" make you feel better. They made me feel a LOT better. Moms, disciplining children is a hard and difficult challenge that needs to be worked on constantly and consistently. Don't be a passive parent; commit yourself to being involved with your children. Be a parent who lovingly takes charge.

 *Stress Busters!*

Moms, I know just how stressful life can be when your children won't listen to you and your discipline doesn't seem to have any effect on them. Try some of these stress busters and see if you don't experience some sense of relief from stress.

- ☀ Create a set of rules and give over the responsibility for enforcing them to your husband. Dad's sometimes have a way of standing their ground that makes children obey. If you are a single mom, ask a relative or good friend to help you stick with your plan.

- ☀ For younger children, create a chart and use fun stickers to record any time your little ones listen to you. Let them pick a prize when they have earned 20 stickers.

- ☀ For your teens, make a contract that states that if they follow the family rules for one week, you will reward them with something they really want (concert tickets come to mind!).

❀ Lower your expectations. You just can't do every thing every day, mom. Ask your husband to help you with disciplinary issues that are especially stressful. Husbands really do want to help, but they can't read our minds.

# Bringing It Home

The main points we have covered in this chapter on being organized about disciplining our children are as follows:

❀ We show our love when we set boundaries, enforce rules with consequences, and discipline our children in love.

❀ Children need us to instill in them an unconditional sense of Acceptance, Belonging, and Competence.

❀ The example we set as moms greatly influences the behavior of our children.

# Plan of Action

For our sixth step to becoming a more organized mom we have focused on the need to "Discipline Your Children in Love." What kind of parent do you want to be regarding the way you discipline your children? How do you want to get there, with God's help? Now look back at your response to Question #5 in the "Personal Inventory" section. Having read this chapter and thought about the ways you discipline your children, do you still agree with what you wrote for Question #5 and the order of importance you gave your ideas? If you do, then complete the sentence below by writing in your #1 choice. Or, create a new #1 choice based on all that you've learned in this chapter.

With God's help I want to _____.

I think I will have to change _____
in order to make this happen. I'm ready to step out in faith with God and make this change, so I can discipline my children in love.

*The world tells our children that siblings and parents
are not cool to be with. As the God-appointed spiritual leaders
of our children, we must begin very early to counteract
this secular psychology with godly wisdom.*

## Step 7
# Manage Your Work and Work Your Finances

**"Make it your ambition to lead a quiet life, to mind your own business and to work with your hands . . . so that you will not be dependent on anybody."**
**—1 Thessalonians 4:11–12**

have the feeling that almost every mom who reads the title of this chapter probably thinks to herself, "Manage my work? All I *do* is work!" Yes, whether we work inside or outside the home, every mom is a working mom. You might have heard the old saying, "Man works from sun to sun; woman's work is never none!"

The ability to manage our workload is where the real payoff for becoming a more organized mom becomes evident. If we work without a plan and without an organized process, we end up feeling discouraged, tired, burned out, and unable to be the mom our children need. But if we work with an organized plan, we can accomplish most of what we need to do each day in our at-home job as well as our outside-the-home job. When we are organized, the level of stress we feel drops, we can accomplish more, we are better able to care for our children, and our whole family benefits.

One would think that, with all the conveniences we have in the twenty-first century, women wouldn't have to work as hard as they do. However, the opposite is true. Women today work harder and longer than our foremothers. For one thing, women live much longer than they used to. And because today there are more divorces and remarriages, a woman might be raising a two-year-old and a twenty-year-old at the same time. If she's a single mom, she may be taking care of an elderly parent at the same time she is raising her teenage daughter alone. If a woman is divorced and remarried, she may be raising children who are "hers, his, and ours," all while trying to bring in an income. Women now hold positions of authority and work in careers that were previously closed to them. So many moms these days work at some type of job, drive the children to every type of activity imaginable, and are still expected to cook and clean as if we were home all day! On top of all that, most of us do not have extended family close by to help us, as our mothers and grandmothers once did. Moms, we are trying to wear so many hats: we're beginning to lose our identity as mothers, and our sanity.

One statistic that surprised me is that, in 1969, 68% of all women worked outside the home. Today that figure has risen to 80%, with the majority increase being mothers with young children. Moms run to work, run back home for this or that school function for their children, and then run back to work. The result is that our health, our marriage and families, our relationships with friends and neighbors, instructional times with our children, and our sense of inner peace are all greatly compromised.

Since *every* mom is a working mom in some capacity—whether at home with your children or working part to full time outside the home—I pray you will find ways to balance what is best for you with what is best for your family. In this chapter we'll discuss several ideas that might help restore a bit of sanity and balance to your life, such as finding a job with more flexible time, learning to delegate more, working different hours than your husband, finding a home-based job, or working longer hours in fewer days. The key word in this chapter is "balance." All of us, at some point in our lives, will be working for an income. It's just a fact of life. But successfully fulfilling all our different responsibilities while earning an income takes consistent, hard work; it's almost like learning to do a juggler's balancing act.

I believe we need to begin saying "No" to activities and "Yes" to a simpler lifestyle. What I mean is that if your child's soccer coach wants her to practice every night, tell him or her "No." One or two nights a week should be plenty (they still have the games to play). If your own volunteer activities meet mostly on school nights and regularly prevent you from preparing dinner or being with your family, perhaps you need to drop some of these activities. If one of your children is asked to be part of a traveling sports team, consider whether or not the cost of being gone many weekends, let alone the travel expenses, are worth it to your family. If your teenager decides to get a job and ends up being away from home every school night, ask him to reconsider what priorities are most important for him and his family at this stage in his life. As a society, we have shifted the focus of our lives away from children and family to activities outside the home. Childhood passes all too quickly: balance your time between you and your children, and others.

Over the course of my life I've been a career woman, a stay-at-home mom, and a working single mom. I *know* it's hard to get it all together and get it all done! I understand the frustrations and hard-ships of juggling the laundry, the shopping, the cooking, the cleaning . . . on top of meeting your own needs and those of your children. And we all need to sleep sometime! Hopefully, this chapter will give you a few ideas about how your approach to your work and your money can help you become a more organized mom.

Reread the verse cited at the beginning of this chapter. If we work hard, we will not be as dependent on others, because we will be working and providing finances, meals, etc., for our family. Work and money are always connected, thus in this chapter we discuss managing our finances and managing our work.

*He is richest who is content with least.*

—Socrates

# Personal Inventory

Getting a handle on our finances is essential if we are to become more organized moms. If we are confident about the way we manage our resources and our work has a positive impact on our lives, then we feel less stress and are better able to care for ourselves and our families. When we aren't able to manage the money we earn, the stress of being in debt and working without any real benefit is extremely discouraging and frustrating.

Making money, spending money, and saving money can be a very emotionally charged and stressful issue in a marriage. Look back on how you were raised. If your parents were big savers, you probably are too. But if you married a man who never had a savings account and sees no need for one, then the two of you could have problems in this area. You need to be on the same wavelength as your spouse, so that together the two of you can manage your own finances well, and teach your children how to manage their own future incomes.

Please understand that the *amount* of money you have is not what is important. It's the way you *manage* the amount of money you have that counts. That's why some people who win the lottery end up filing for bankruptcy: they think money is the answer to all their problems and do not realize that the way they manage the amount of money they have—whether great or small—either creates or solves problems.

Before doing this chapter's "Personal Inventory," get out your checkbook and your most recent bank and credit card statements. Now you're ready to take an honest look at how you handle your money.

1. When it comes to money in general, I . . . (Check all that apply.)

   ❑ pinch pennies because I worry about not having enough

   ❑ overspend on my credit cards

   ❑ find it impossible to save each month

   ❑ allow someone else to control my money

   ❑ pay only the minimum amount due on credit cards

   ❑ decide not to tithe

   ❑ set a budget and save, give, and spend without fear

   ❑ invest my money

   ❑ plan for retirement, loss of a job, illness, children's education, etc.

   ❑ spend a windfall such as a tax refund or a bonus check

   ❑ save so much that I can't enjoy small luxuries such as eating dinner out or taking in a movie

   ❑ buy just to buy or to keep up with others

   ❑ balance my checking account each month

   ❑ pay my bills on time

2. Who makes the important financial decisions for your family?

   ❑ Me

   ❑ My husband

   ❑ Financial Advisor

   ❑ Other _____

3. Think about the *little* expenses you incur every day or every week (that daily latte on the way to work, for instance). List those expenses here, as well as how much each one costs.

_____ $_____      _____ $_____

_____ $_____      _____ $_____

_____ $_____      _____ $_____

Challenge: For one month, try putting the money you would have spent on these items into a glass jar. At the end of the month count up the money you saved and take it to the bank. Now use the worksheet below to see where your money is going each month.

### Budget Worksheet

| Category | Monthly Budget Amount | Monthly Actual Amount | Difference Between Actual and Budget |
|---|---|---|---|
| **Income:** | | | |
| Wages Earned | | | |
| Bonuses Earned | | | |
| Interest Income | | | |
| Capital Gains Income | | | |
| Dividend Income | | | |
| Miscellaneous Income | | | |
| **Total Income:** | | | |
| | | | |
| **Expenses:** | | | |
| Mortgage or Rent | | | |
| Utilities (heating, electricity, water, garbage pick-up) | | | |
| Telephone | | | |
| Television (incl. cable expenses) | | | |
| Home Owner/Renter's Insurance | | | |
| Home Repairs/Maintenance | | | |
| Car Payments | | | |

| Category | Monthly Budget Amount | Monthly Actual Amount | Difference Between Actual and Budget |
|---|---|---|---|
| **Expenses (continued):** | | | |
| Auto Insurance | | | |
| Auto Repair/Maintenance/Gas/Fees | | | |
| Other Transportation Expenses (tolls, bus, subway, cab, etc.) | | | |
| Child Care | | | |
| Computer Expenses (incl. Internet use fees) | | | |
| Entertainment/Recreation (incl. vacation expenses) | | | |
| Groceries | | | |
| Toiletries/Household Products | | | |
| Clothing | | | |
| Eating Out | | | |
| Gifts/Donations/Tithe | | | |
| Healthcare Insurance (medical/dental/life) | | | |
| Hobbies | | | |
| Interest Expenses (mortgage, credit cards, fees) | | | |
| Magazines/Newspapers | | | |
| Federal Income Tax | | | |
| State Income Tax | | | |
| Social Security/Medicare Tax | | | |
| Personal Property Tax | | | |
| Pets | | | |
| Miscellaneous Expenses | | | |
| **TOTAL EXPENSES** | | | |
| **NET INCOME (INCOME LESS EXPENSES)** | | | |

If an expense is incurred more or less on a regular basis, but not monthly, then calculate and include it in the Monthly Budget Amount. For instance, if your automobile insurance is billed every six months, convert it to a monthly expense by dividing the six-month premium by six (a worksheet similar to this one can be found at *http://financialplan.about.com*).

4. Now that you've examined yourself under the financial microscope, have you thought of some monetary habits you'd like to change? In the spaces below, write three habits that you want to change, so you can get a better grip on the family's finances. Then number these according to order of priority.

#____  _____

#____  _____

#____  _____

Moms, now you know where your money goes each month, which can be both encouraging and discouraging! But remember, this is a way to help you get back on track with your finances. So even if the picture looks discouraging, be encouraged because now you can change it for the better.

## *The Rule of 72*

If you want a quick way to see how much time it would take for your investments to double in value, you can calculate this easily by using what is called "The Rule of 72." Divide your estimated rate of return (say 8%) into 72 and you've got the years it will take to double your money, assuming your investments are earning compound interest.

$$\frac{72}{8} \quad = \quad 9$$

(rate of return)    (years for money to double)

### Example

| | | |
|---|---|---|
| If you open an IRA at age . . . | 25 | 45 |
| With a monthly contribution of . . . | $60 | $200 |
| Then stop saving at age . . . | 65 | 65 |
| Your total contribution will be . . . | $28,800 | $48,000 |
| Your savings may grow to . . . | $379,445 | $151,874 |

---

*Beware of little expenses. A small leak will sink a great ship.*

—Benjamin Franklin

---

 ## Everybody Wins!

It has been said that the number one reason for divorce in America is problems that arise over money. This is a huge incentive to become organized and mature about the way we handle our finances. When we work hard at our jobs and handle the money we earn as responsible stewards, then we have greater confidence and trust that the Lord will provide for all our needs; and we win respect for ourselves! But more importantly, our children win as they learn by our example how to be responsible, trustworthy, and competent in handling money. Our children will be working most of their lives. What a gift we give them if we can teach them the importance of being organized in their work and finances!

*What I've Learned*

I have been through every stage of working. Before my first daughter was born, I was working, and then I quit just before she was born. When she was little, I worked three part-time jobs from home and one job at a gym: I embroidered panty diaper covers for a baby specialty shop, worked as a bookkeeper in my father and brother's family business, made real-estate phone calls, and taught children gymnastics one or two afternoons a week. When we moved to Littleton, Colorado, I was so busy relocating that I didn't continue some of these, but instead became active in Bible studies, school activities, singing, etc. When my younger daughter was six, I began public speaking, writing, and teaching a Bible study, but I was still basically at home. It wasn't until my marriage of twenty-five years ended that I began to work outside the home again.

My younger daughter was fourteen years old when my husband and I divorced. I was frantic to find a job that would allow me to take her to school before work and pick her up after work. (We weren't on a bus line, so I was her only transportation.) Moms, let me tell you, I was on my face before the Lord, praying for Him to find me a job that would accommodate school hours. I became a substitute teacher, but the pay was low and irregular. One day I was so desperate I decided to look in the Sunday newspaper (I didn't think good jobs would be there). I saw an ad for a job there, called for more information, and set up an interview. Two weeks later, the boss still wasn't sure about hiring me part time. He had never hired part time before, and since this was a sales position, it required full-time hours to get the work done. But the job was with a Christian publisher and I would be selling to Christian schools and churches. A perfect fit! (Remember the verse, "Ask and it shall be given to you"?) Finally, I said to him, "Sir, I need this job and I have to have these hours for my daughter right now. Could you just give me a trial for thirty days, and if I haven't proven myself to you, I'll leave?"

Well, I'm very happy to report that I have now been working for this company for over three years. I love my job, and I foresee a great future working there. The other wonderful aspect is that whenever I have a public speaking engagement, my boss understands this priority and lets me take time off for it. I work four days a week, six hours a day, but because the job is in sales I'm able to increase my salary through commissions and bonuses. Now you tell me, does God answer prayer?! We were able to continue my daughter's routine as it had been and I was able to be with her at home in the afternoons, and this eased the stressful effects of divorce for both of us.

I'm sure that some of you reading this are trying to survive perilous circumstances right now. *God will see you through.* I literally thought I was going to die; my depression and sense of loss were so severe that there were days when I couldn't get out of bed. But I had a daughter who still needed a mom, a home life, meals, clean clothes, and a ride to school. At first I would take her to school and then crawl back into bed, but over time I grew stronger, physically as well as emotionally. I *never* thought I would be able to support myself or be a single mom—nor did I want to! But I have learned that we moms can and will do what we have to do for ourselves and our children. We pick ourselves up, grab the Lord's hand, and keep going. I promise you that your strength and hard work will be the best example you can give your children about trusting God and persevering in life. Life is always changing—it's never predictable and at times it's very difficult—but God's providential love and grace are always there to sustain us.

 *Try This . . .*

Below is one family's story that was published in *The Fact File,* an information letter published by the Christian Broadcasting Network, entitled "Two Incomes and Still Broke?" The point is that it's not how much you make, but how much you keep that is important. Are you finding that the extra money you earn is "disappearing" to pay for those hidden job expenses created by the second income, expenses such as child care and income taxes? Child care is often the biggest expense, sometimes eating up every dollar of the second income. And if you aren't careful, income taxes can suddenly soar upward in a shocking fashion. Even a very limited second job can push the family's income over into a higher tax bracket, where both jobs are taxed more.

> *Cory Schaff, a young policeman who has a wife, a son, a baby, a mortgage, and two car payments, wanted to better himself, so he began taking and paying for a full load of classes at Savannah State College. To pay the bills, he's been working two part-time jobs along with his full-time police job. Yet he still didn't feel there was enough money. So Cory's wife, Morgan, decided she had to go to work. She had an offer for a full-time job, but the hours were the same as Cory's police job. Taking the job would have meant hiring a full-time baby sitter, which would cost them about $500 every week: "My paycheck wouldn't even cover day care for a week," remarked Morgan. So instead, Morgan took a part-time job, helping at one of Savannah's most chic restaurants. She's making a little less money, but getting to keep almost all of it because her hours are such that Cory can be with the kids when she's working and vise versa.*

Linda Kelley, the author of this article, suggests that Morgan's decision might be the answer for many full-time working women who are suffering and falling behind:

*Only 4% of women want to work full-time. And they're getting tired of that double-shift: eight hours at the office and then coming home to almost as many hours at home. When I'm home, I have the time to do a lot more, even if it's cooking or sewing . . . and when I'm working, I don't.*

One statistic from this article that really shocked me was that studies suggest many men might make more money if their wives decided to work less: "Men with MBAs earn 25% more if their wives stay at home, and men get raises 20% higher if their wives don't work outside of the home." Kelley believes that modern couples need to really study their finances and look very carefully at the benefits they're getting—or losing!—from both partners running the rat race: more and more couples are beginning to realize that having two paychecks and a good quality of life aren't necessarily connected.

After reading the story of this family, how would you rate the benefits of your working? Could a second income actually be *costing* you money and unnecessary stress? Take time to think and pray over the different options you might have, and seek the counsel of a wise friend who can suggest options you might not have considered. Then, do the math. You may find that some of the choices you're making can be changed, and this alone may save your family a considerable amount of money, and you less stress!

Moms, the goal of this book is to help you experience less stress and more joy in your life as a mom, for when that happens, your family will reap so many benefits. Below are a few tips to help you in the area of finances:

- ☼ Spend less than you earn. This is the #1 solution to every money problem.

- ☼ Pay off credit card debt immediately! It costs a small fortune to pay this off when high interest accrues every month. Pay the debts off, and then save what you used to pay toward debt. It's like getting an instant savings account!

- ☼ Track all of your small expenses for one month. You know, the ones you think don't amount to much. It's fun to go through the drive-through and get one of those cute little coffee drinks, but you could easily be spending over $1,200 a year drinking just one coffee a day on the way to work! At the end of the month you'll be amazed at how much money you save by not spending this way.

❀ For help with managing your finances, check with your church, the Chamber of Commerce, or the Yellow Pages for free financial counseling services in your area. Or, call the Christian Broadcast Network's National Counseling Center at 1-800-759-0700 and request their "Guide to Financial Freedom." They also have a website, *www.cbn.com.* Go to their Personal Finance page under Channel Options.

❀ Make an appointment with your local bank or find a reputable financial planner, such as USA Tax Advisors Incorporated (1-800-460-9909), Merrill Lynch, or UBS Paine Webber. If your bank does not take your inquiry seriously, change banks! You must find a place that is trustworthy and cares about your personal financial situation, especially if you are a single mom.

❀ Read books by Jane Bryant Quinn and Suze Orman, who teach women how to manage their money.

❀ For stock and investment information, read Andrew Tobias's *The Only Investment Guide You'll Ever Need.*

❀ Larry Burkett's books on finances are great to get you started and keep you on track: *Debt Free Living, The Family Financial Workbook,* and *Your Child and Money.*

❀ Be careful and knowledgeable when buying stocks. Don't speculate, but invest in stocks for the long haul via no-load, low-expense, mutual funds. If you are over age fifty, check into the equity annuity market. The gains are based on the stock market, but you can never lose a penny! I personally believe this is the safest and best place to invest your money. But don't invest your money until you are really sure what to do with it.

- Stop trying to keep up with the Joneses. Live beneath your means, and invest what's left over in a short-term savings account, a Roth IRA, or annuities.

- Make wise purchases by thinking ahead. Buy clothes for next year when they go on sale this year, and buy Christmas presents all year long so you won't go into debt in December.

- Set goals and make a budget to attain them. Most people retire with nothing, says financial writer Venita Van Caspel Harris, "not because they plan to fail, but because they fail to plan."

- Shop for your groceries online, using services such as Stop & Shop's Peapod, to avoid impulse buying.

- Clip coupons each week before you do your shopping. You'll be amazed at how much money you save.

Every mom is a working mom; we just work in different ways. We've looked at our finances, knowing that if we get them in order, we will have extra money for our families and ourselves, and hopefully reduce the level of stress we feel. Now let's find ways to structure our lives so that we can wear all our hats with confidence, peace, and joy. Let's learn how we can mesh our home demands with our work demands. We can't do everything every day, but as we become more organized, we will be able to do a lot more each week.

- Plan, plan, plan. If you have a job, even if it's one where you work out of a home office, you still need to plan all you have to do in order to get your work done. As I mentioned in chapter 2, scheduling our time and setting our priorities are the keys to accomplishing our tasks. So get a calendar and begin to make lists. And remember this key point: as you schedule time for work and time for home, make sure you schedule some time just for you each and every day. Whether it's a walk, a bubble bath, a phone call to a friend or family member, a nap, or just sitting quietly and reading, I promise that if you make time for yourself, you will begin to develop a strong sense of peace that will transform your family.

⚜ Make lists of everything you have to do each day and each week, from going to work to cleaning the house, driving the children, shopping and cooking, laundry, doing school or office homework. Make sure you also make a list of things you *want* to do each week.

⚜ Divide your days on the calendar into job work hours and home work hours, and plot these on your calendar. You might want to designate your work hours in different colors. As you are plotting the hours (and they might be different each day if you work part time), take the list of chores you have to do and begin to insert them into available time slots.

⚜ As you insert your chores into the time slots on your calendar, you will begin to see realistically how to get everything done. No, you can't do everything, every day! But you can clean one day, cook only a couple of days a week and use leftovers for the other few days, and wash clothes each day at a particular time when you know you will be home, etc.

⚜ If you realize that you simply cannot do everything you have to do, then it's time for a readjustment. If you cannot schedule time to plan the evening meal, time to spend with your family, and some time alone for yourself, then you are doing too much. It's time to downsize and to begin to say "No!" And moms, we all have to have help. Now is the time to delegate responsibilities to others: children can and should help; husbands can and should help! And if you are working part time or full time outside the home or have several children under the age of five years, then you need to get someone to help you with the household chores. If money is an issue, then very sweetly show your husband your "To Do" list and ask what part he would like to be his responsibility. It's crazy even to think you can do it all. Also think about organizing a carpool with neighbors, asking teenagers to mow your lawn (they might be cheaper than a landscape or lawn service, and then you wouldn't have to do it!), or joining a babysitting co-op.

☀ If you are finding yourself just too stressed from your full-time job, then look into ways that you can either cut some of your hours and work part time, or maybe just quit for a while. I know this next statement will make me very unpopular with some of you moms, but if you have babies or young children, then the best place for you to be is *with them as much as possible.* If you are able to work hours while your husband can keep the children, that is a better solution than daycare, but not a great solution. Babies and young children need you! Your husband needs you when he comes home. And you need "a you" who is not fatigued, overly stressed, and worn out. If you feel that you just have to work, try to find a job with fewer hours or more flexibility. Or, are there expenses you could eliminate, so that you don't have to work at this time? Could you move to a smaller home, sell your car for a less expensive one, drop a club membership?

☀ Consider working out of your home. Read *101 Best Home-Based Businesses for Women* by Priscilla Y. Huff. From choosing a business that's right for you to marketing your product, this book might be a good first step toward working for yourself, from home.

Perhaps after trying some of these tips you may be able to make adjustments that allow you to change to part-time work, or even quit your job while your children are young. Keep your ears open for possibilities and your heart open as you pray. God knows your financial and work situation even better than you do. He wants us to come to Him for *everything,* and that includes what to do with our time, work, and life. If you feel that you have to work, then ask the Lord to show you a job that will accommodate the schedules of your children and husband. If you feel that you need to stop work, then ask the Lord to show you how to manage without that income. There are jobs available in our neighborhoods (probably several home-based businesses or someone who has a home office and needs some office help); in our schools (teacher aids, substitute teachers, which I have done); in our churches (even if they don't have a job for you, they are a great place to network); in our hospitals; or in any of the businesses near your home.

## *Top 10 Favorite Shopping Websites*

1. *www.mysimon.com—searches the Internet for the best price*
2. *www.half.com—half-price books, videos, CDs, and more*
3. *www.ebay.com—best auction site*
4. *www.travelocity.com—great prices on airline tickets*
5. *www.priceline.com—good values on car rentals, hotels, and airfares*
6. *www.estyle.com—up to 75% off brand-name clothing*
7. *www.bizrate.com—great savings on apparel, sports equipment, etc.*
8. *www.buy.com—computer and software values*
9. *www.scentiments.com—discounted fragrances*
10. *www.toysrus.com—save up to 60% at this toy outlet*

*—Today's Christian Woman* magazine

 # *Set a Good Example*

Setting a good example for our children in the management of finances and work is extremely important. Without a good work ethic and a plan for financial stewardship, our children could very easily waste their lives. The Bible says that when we are faithful in little things, then God entrusts us with greater things. So, as your children become responsible in little things, they will begin to develop skills and ethical habits that influence their future education, jobs, careers, friendships, and marriage.

Moms, don't put your financial head in the sand! No matter who makes the most money, you and your husband need to work together when making important financial decisions. You have just as much net worth as your husband does, no matter what your "job description" looks like: your worth is priceless! Go to your local library and check out books on how to manage money. If your husband will not let you have any say when it comes to money, then go to a Christian counselor or a financial advisor who can suggest options for you. If you are an older mom, sit down with your husband and set up a folder that addresses every financial question you might have, in case your husband dies before you do, which is often the case.

Moms, also understand the importance of giving. When most people think about wealth, they think about money. But true wealth is what makes up the substance of our lives: peace, joy, love, family, stability, faith, contentment, and friends. If we go through life thinking we will never have enough, we will begin to hold too tightly to what we do have. And if we never have the faith to begin giving, we will never experience what God desires to come into our open hands. I love the story of the Widow's Mite in Mark 12:41–44. Jesus teaches His disciples about true giving, using a poor widow as an example. Many rich men were putting great sums of money into the temple treasury, when along came a very poor widow who "put in all she had." Her contribution amounted to only a fraction of a penny. But Jesus said to His disciples, "I tell you the truth, this poor widow has put more into the treasury than all the others. They gave out of their wealth; but she, out of her poverty, put in everything—all she had to live on." We can draw at least three lessons from the widow's example: (1) Jesus praises those who give because their focus is on God and not the benefits God might provide; (2) God can use anything we give to Him (remember the little boy with two fish and five loaves of bread?); and (3) God wants us to give Him our all. Not the rent money! But our attitude should be one of great joy in giving back to our Lord.

God loves us so much that He gave up His most precious, treasured, only Son for us. It is this example of giving that should compel us to want to give as much as we can throughout our whole lives. God wants us to give. That's why He mentions tithing and giving throughout His Word. He wants us to give because of the way giving affects our hearts. He can't bless a closed-up, selfish soul.

When we give to others out of our desire to give back, our giving comes from an inspired place deep within us and reveals our trust and faith in One who is greater than our paychecks or raises. How much should you give? You are the only one who can determine that, although God says that we should give a tenth of our income. I believe we should give our tithe out of our first paycheck, at the beginning of each month and before any other bills are paid. I also believe we should give on a regular basis. If you are in credit card debt, this will be quite difficult. *But start tithing anyway.* God promises to bless us, in fact He asks us to test Him in this: "Bring the whole tithe into the storehouse, so that there may be food in My house, and test Me now in this," says the LORD of hosts, "if I will not open for you the windows of heaven and pour out for you a blessing until it overflows" (Malachi 3:10 NASB). I believe with all my heart that trusting the Lord with our finances will multiply the blessings He wants to bestow on us.

Some of you may be thinking that you have so much work to do that you don't even want to think about finances. I can understand that so well. I get so tired of paying all the bills, etc. I also think that men really are not aware of everything we do every day. I hope this next story will make you laugh!

---

*A man was sick and tired of going to work every day while his wife stayed home. He wanted her to see what he went through so he prayed, "Dear Lord: I go to work every day and put in eight hours while my wife merely stays home. I want her to*

*know what I go through, so please allow her body to switch
with mine for a day. Amen."*

*God, in His infinite wisdom, granted the man's wish. The
next morning, sure enough, the man awoke as a woman. He
didn't want to get out of bed, but he arose, cooked breakfast for
his mate, awakened the kids, set out their school clothes, fed
them breakfast, made and packed their lunches, drove them to
school, came back home to pick up the dry cleaning and take it
to the cleaners, then stopped at the bank to make a deposit,
went grocery shopping, and drove back home where he put
away the groceries, paid some bills, balanced the checkbook,
and sifted through the calendar to see when there might be time
to schedule everyone's annual dental checkup. While home, the
phone kept ringing with requests to help at school, bake cookies,
find a craft project for the Brownie meeting, and pick up
another child after school. He then cleaned the cat's litter box,
because litter and "stuff" was everywhere, and he bathed the
dog. By now it was already 1:00 p.m., and he still hadn't had
time to make lunch but he hurried to make the beds, do some
laundry, vacuum, dust, and mop the kitchen floor, where the
spilled milk and Cheerios were still at flood level.*

*Quickly, he rushed back to school to pick up the kids, and got
into an argument with them on the way home: "How could
that happen within one minute of them getting in the car?" he
wondered. He provided great snacks for the kids, and couldn't
understand why they kept demanding something else. He
finally got them to start their homework, and then he set up the
ironing board in front of the TV. But he couldn't get much
ironing done because he realized that if he didn't start dinner
at that point, it would be too late to eat. So he began peeling
potatoes and washing vegetables for salad; he cut the skin and
fat off of the chicken, snapped some fresh green beans, and set
the table. When his mate came home, she couldn't understand
why he was so tired, tense, in a hurry, and ruffled-looking.*

*After supper he cleaned the kitchen, ran the dishwasher, folded
the laundry, bathed the kids, read them stories and tried to
teach them a little about values and morals; then he put them
to bed. At 9:00 p.m. he was exhausted, and even though his
daily responsibilities still weren't finished he went to bed,*

*where he was expected to be exciting and intimate, which he managed to get through without complaint.*

*The next morning he awoke and immediately knelt by the bed and said, "Lord, I don't know what I was thinking. I was so wrong to envy my wife's being able to stay home all day. Please, oh please, let us trade back!"*

*The Lord replied, "My son, I feel you have learned your lesson and I will be happy to change things back to the way they were. You'll just have to wait nine months, though. You got pregnant last night.*

*— Author Unknown*

© BIL KEANE, INC. KING FEATURES SYNDICATE

 *Stress Busters!*

Needless to say, moms, we need a way to take a break from all the stress produced by money and work demands. Here are some quick, easy, and inexpensive tips to help every mom at any age:

144

- ❁ Walk away from the stress! Leave the kitchen, the sewing machine, the computer, etc., and go outside for a walk in the sunshine.

- ❁ Do something for someone who is less fortunate than you. When we do for others, it releases "feel-good" hormones!

- ❁ Count your blessings. I really mean this. Either speak or write down your blessings in a journal every single day.

- ❁ Perhaps you are trying to do too much. Set new, more realistic goals, delegate more, and learn to say "No."

- ❁ Take mini-vacations. Perhaps your mother or a good friend could keep the children for a day or an overnight, so you can rest and/or be with your husband. If you work, take Friday off so you have longer weekends.

- ❁ Identify the time of the day that is most difficult for you, the time when you are really beginning to feel tired and burned out. Think of something simple and enjoyable you can do to boost your energy level at that time of day.

 ## *Bringing It Home*

Moms, remember that the lessons we teach our children about managing finances and work are enormously powerful. This seventh step, "Manage Your Work and Work your Finances" is probably one of the most important in helping you become a more organized mom. When we become organized enough to handle our work and finances well, we discover that these attributes spill over into the other areas of our lives. And, as your workload and finances are brought into balance, your self-esteem will soar!

*Want to see how your children's attitudes change when they are spending their own money? Try one of my favorite tricks. Next time you go to the mall, give your kids $10 each to spend, but* *tell them you expect change. Trust me, you won't get much back. On your next visit, give them $10 again. But this time, tell them they can keep the change. You'll be amazed by how much less they spend.*

— Jonathan Clements, *Wall Street Journal,* October 22, 2003

Giving our children money, without teaching them how to earn, save, give, and spend it responsibly, is one of the most detrimental things we can do. They need to learn how to earn, save, give, and spend money. That way, when they leave your home for the great big world, they won't fall flat on their empty wallets!

Moms, when we are organized and responsible and then teach our children to be this way, we truly help the next generation succeed. The main points made in this chapter are:

- ☀ Remember that God is our source for everything.

- ☀ Track your money and your spending, along with a savings plan.

- ☀ God will show you the work that is best for you and your family, if you ask.

In the Bible, the word *love* is mentioned 714 times, *pray* 371 times, and *believe* 272 times, but *money* is mentioned 2,162 times!

 *Plan of Action*

For our seventh step to becoming a more organized mom we have focused on how to "Manage Your Work and Work Your Finances." What have you learned about yourself, how you handle money, and why you work? What are some things you would like to start doing to help you manage your work and money better, with God's help? Look back at your response to Question #4 in the "Personal Inventory" section for this chapter. Do you still agree with what you wrote and the order of importance you gave your three ideas? If you do, then complete the sentence below by writing in your #1 choice. Or, create a new #1 choice based on all that you've learned in this chapter.

With God's help I want to _____.

I think I will have to change _____ in order to make this happen. I'm ready to step out in faith with God and make this change so that I can better manage my finances and work, putting God first in this aspect of my life.

Moms, don't forget that whether you are currently at home with your children, working part time, or working full time outside the home, you are a working mom. Every day there will be hurdles to overcome and new paths to seek out. There will be days of great joy and others of deep sadness. But through it all, the Lord is holding your hand and guiding you through: "He gently leads those that have young" (Isaiah 40:11). I pray that you will rest in this promise from the Lord as you work for Him.

## Step 8

# Recover Your Sense of Self

**"Therefore, if anyone is in Christ,
he is a new creation; the old has gone,
the new has come!"
—2 Corinthians 5:17**

Scientists report that when women shop in the grocery store, their eyes glaze over, as if they are in a trance. Personally, I think our eyes look that way because they haven't been closed long enough in sleep! Also, we have been summoned "Mom" so many times and performed so many jobs in that role that at times we can't even remember our name, date of birth, or where we parked the car! Sometimes when I reflect back on the day I gave birth to my first daughter, I see that day as the beginning of a slow and subtle process that ended with the loss of my own sense of self, *as a person.*

Who are we moms, really? We have so many different titles: mother, daughter, granddaughter, sister, wife, aunt, cousin, grandmother, stepmother, and mother/daughter/sister-in-law, to name a few. Given all these different titles and the roles they suggest, are you still the same person you were before marriage and motherhood? I'd have to answer, "Well, yes . . . and no."

I say "Yes" because I still have the same DNA I had when I was born, and I still have the same parents, family heritage, and childhood memories. But I say "No" because marriage and the birth of my children created so many new and different desires, goals, needs, wants, and thoughts, that sometimes I scarcely feel I am the same person I was before all this happened. With each of life's seasons, each loss and each joy, I have changed. And I don't mean I have changed only emotionally; I have changed physically and spiritually as well—all of me has changed! Those things that I thought were important when I was eighteen don't even give me pause now, and the spiritual dimension of my life has become much more important than the physical. I love Paul's words in 2 Corinthians 4:16 (NASB), "Therefore we do not lose heart, but though our outer man is decaying, yet our inner man is being renewed day by day," because these words help me focus on the eternal, rather than the temporal.

Moms, if you feel like you have lost your identity and sense of self, please don't lose heart! I know many of you reading this feel you have lost your identity and the best parts of your self to "the mothering years." Believe me, I know what it feels like to take a step back and wonder, "Where is that teenager or college student who never needed to sleep, was so smart and so 'with it,' and always looked so good?" Well, let me tell you, she still lives right where you are; she still lives inside you. We just have to dig her out!

One of my purposes in writing this book is to help you become more organized as a mom, so you and your families will thrive in life. But a second purpose is to walk alongside you on the journey, and let you know that you are a wonderful person. When the twins won't sleep, your teenager won't talk to you, and your husband wonders when you'll get your figure back, I want you to know that you are precious in the eyes of our Lord. You are just as precious right now as you were the day He created you.

Each one of us—even those who have nannies, cooks, and maids—feels at times that we are inadequate, unloved, and a failure. Motherhood is the hardest job there is, because we have to die to ourselves for the sake of others. Some of you have been living in survival mode for so long—being the person others wanted or needed you to be—that you're not sure who you are now, and you can't even remember what your dreams used to be. Let's begin to resurrect the person who "got lost in Aisle 3"! It just takes a little time, a little planning, and a whole lot of want-to. As you read this chapter, keep an open mind and heart, and get ready to recover your sense of self.

*Understand your personality.* The first step in resurrecting your unique, real self is to understand your personality type. I had the opportunity one time to be in a workshop with Florence Littauer, a best-selling author, public speaker, and the founder of CLASServices. Her book *Personality Plus* sold over one million copies. If you read that one, you might also want to check out her two newest books, *Personality Plus for Couples* and *Personality Plus for Parents.* The fundamental thought that underlies each of these books is that each of us has a particular type of personality, or a mixture of them. Knowing your personality type helps you understand your most natural way of relating to others, your basic desires, and what helps you feel emotionally secure.

Littauer describes four personality types. See if you especially relate to the desires and emotional needs of one of these.

- ❀ Sanguine: Desires fun! Needs attention, affection, approval, and activity with people.

- ❀ Choleric: Desires control! Needs appreciation for achievements, opportunity for leadership, participation in decisions, and something to control.

- ❀ Melancholy: Desires perfection! Needs sensitivity, stability, support, space, and silence.

- ❀ Phlegmatic: Desires peace! Needs times of quiet, reduced stress, feelings of worth, and relaxation.

I highly suggest you read more about these personality types in order to understand yourself and the members of your family. Often, marriages are mended and children change when we begin to understand one another's personality type, because this enables us to understand one another's behavior. Other resources to consider are Dr. Kevin Leman's best-selling book, *The Birth Order Book,* which explains how our birth order can affect and determine our personality type. Another one of my favorite books about different personality types in children is *The Treasure Tree,* by John and Cindy Trent and Gary and Norma Smalley.

As you seek to identify your personality type, remember that God made you and He loves you just the way you are: "LORD, you have searched me and you know me," says Psalm 139:1. Since God gives each of us unique characteristics and traits, making a commitment to be the "real you" leads to a true sense of peace and purpose in your life. Then you can say, "I praise you because I am fearfully and wonderfully made" (Psalm 139:14).

Remember also that nothing we do or study is as life-changing as prayer: "Trust in the LORD, and do good; dwell in the land, and feed on His faithfulness. Delight yourself also in the LORD, and He shall give you the desires of your heart" (Psalm 37:3–4 NKJV). Let the Lord lead you on this journey of finding yourself. He will be faithful in revealing His will to you, as you put your trust in Him.

*Rekindle your passions, activities, hobbies, talents, and gifts.* Close your eyes and remember the person you were before you had children. How did you occupy your free time? What were your interests, your hobbies? When you "treated" yourself, what did you do and how often? Granted, having a family requires that these things take a somewhat lower priority, but that doesn't mean that we have to give them up completely.

Most of our husbands have not given up those things they enjoyed before the children were born. Many of them still play golf, hunt, or fish. I don't want to put you in a place of conflict with your husband, but sometimes our husbands need a wake-up call so we too can find the time we need for ourselves! I know many husbands who have made great sacrifices so that their wives could go back to school, start a business, or begin a hobby. My father, who was an excellent golfer, stopped playing golf completely so he could be home with my mother. He traveled all week, every week, and Saturday was the only day he could be with us and help her. I so appreciated his thoughtfulness and understanding of what was important in that season of his life.

Something you may not have thought of before is that the more interests you have that are not about your children, the more interesting you will become to your children, and the more your children will respect and obey you. John Rosemond, a family psychologist and author, wrote about a woman who said that being a mother was the most demanding, difficult thing she had ever done: "It sounds like you need to learn how to stop being a mother," he replied. She laughed: "How can someone with three children possibly stop being a mother?" He explained that if motherhood was wearing her out, she was probably doing too much for her children and not nearly enough for herself.

Years ago you may have loved snow skiing, but now your interests may have changed. What interests you now? What hobbies do you have now? Did you know that hobbies have healing power? Experts agree that being an enthusiastic hobbyist is good for you. Hobbies reduce stress, says Alice Domar, director of the Mind/Body Center for Women's Health at Harvard Medical School. They distract you from everyday worries: if you're focused on the pottery you're making, you can't fret about work. And knitting, or anything that requires repetitive motion, elicits the relaxation response, a feeling of overall serenity that lowers blood pressure.

Hobbies provide a calming sense of control. You may not have much control over your workplace, but when you're working on your scrapbooks, you're in charge. You get the credit—and the satisfaction—of a job well done. A Swedish study showed that people who regularly engage in hobbies such as sewing and gardening are less likely to suffer mental decline as they age (this is great news for me, because my children think I've lost my mind). Similar research, reported in the *New England Journal of Medicine* (cited by Shari Caudron in *Reader's Digest*, 2003), found that those who pursue mind-boosting activities such as crossword puzzles lower their risk of developing Alzheimer's disease and other forms of dementia. For moms who are at times isolated, many hobbies provide great opportunities for socializing. From playing bridge to swapping tips with other collectors, engaging with like-minded souls boosts our immunities.

*Remember why you are working.* For those of you who work in a job other than full-time home management, your lack of identity can become much more pronounced and critical. You are trying to bring in an income *and* keep up your family and home. On top of that, you may feel that you still haven't quite found your calling. You have a job but it doesn't bring you the joy or purpose you had hoped for; it's not a vocation. Let's ask some questions that may help you discover the work you were born to do. (You might even think about taking some time off to figure out why you are not happy and how to make some changes.)

Think back to your childhood and what you wanted to be and do when you grew up. Can you turn what you loved to do into a job that can earn you a living? Is it time to find a part-time job so you can have more time for your family and yourself? Many of you moms don't want to work. You want to stay home with your little ones, but you feel that you have to work. Recalculate how much you really make after deducting child care, transportation expenses, the higher taxes you may be paying because you are in a higher income bracket, etc. If selling your car or your house will allow you to stay home, perhaps you and your husband should seriously consider doing this. Your babies and young children need only one thing each day and that is *you.* Pray for God to work a miracle so you can reduce your hours. Your marriage, your family, and your health will become much stronger! If you are a single mom, let's work together in the next section to find a job that will be a blessing to you rather than a frustration. Remember what the flight attendant says at the beginning of each flight? "In case of lack of oxygen, place the yellow mask over your face *first,* and then you can help your family."

Richard Leider, a founding partner of the Inventure Group, a coaching and consulting firm, specializes in helping people find their vocational calling in life. Part of his process includes answering the following questions:

* What are your gifts/talents?
* What are your passions/interests?
* What are your values?
* What work environments are you best suited for?

"Once you know those things, you can discover if where you currently are is where you need to be," says Leider. You may be able to determine your calling just by answering these four questions. Or you may need additional tools and exercises to help you clarify what your gifts and strengths are. Leider's group developed a simple but effective tool called "Calling Cards" to help in discerning these issues. You can learn more about this system at the website, *www.inventuregroup.com.*

I pray that you will discover what God has called you to do. People who find their calling are generally happier, healthier, and live longer than people who stay in jobs they don't like.

*Renew your relationships.* One of the best ways to restore or find your identity is to renew the friendships and important relationships in your life. Remember when you were in Brownies or Girl Scouts and sang, "Make new friends, but keep the old. One is silver and the other gold"? How true this is! A landmark UCLA study entitled "Friendship Among Women," conducted in March 2003, suggests that friendships between women are special because they shape who we are and who we will become. They soothe our tumultuous inner world, fill the emotional gaps in our marriage, and help us remember who we really are.

Friendships with women also help us physically. In fact, scientists now suspect that hanging out with friends can actually counteract the kind of stomach-quivering stress most of us experience on a daily basis. Women respond to stress by releasing a cascade of brain chemicals that causes us to make and maintain friendships with other women: "Until this study was published, scientists generally believed that when people experience stress, they trigger a hormonal cascade that revs the body to either stand and fight or flee as fast as possible," explains Laura Cousin Klein,

Ph.D., now an Assistant Professor of Biobehavioral Health at Penn State University and one of the study's authors. In fact, it seems that when the hormone oxytocin is released as part of a woman's stress response, it buffers the "fight or flight" response and encourages her to tend her children and gather together with other women instead. Since nearly 90% of research studies on stress only focus on males, the discovery that women respond to stress differently from men is a revolutionary finding.

Of course, it may take time for new studies to reveal all the ways that oxytocin encourages us to care for our children and hang out with other women, but the "tend and befriend" notion developed by Drs. Klein and Taylor may explain why women consistently out-live men: "There's no doubt," says Dr. Klein, "that friends are helping us live longer." Friendships also help us live better. We are healthier and function better after a loss, such as the death of a spouse, when we have friends to turn to for love and support.

So don't allow yourself to become too isolated, whether because you're too busy, too tired, or depressed. Stay in contact with your friends and talk about things that matter to both of you. Be honest and supportive of one another. And remember the golden rule of friendship: if you want to *have* a good friend, you need to *be* a good friend.

*Re-think your life goals.* What are you living for? What are you striving for? How will you know if you've been successful? Do you define "success" as having more money, more happiness, a good reputation, social status, or a family? Whose standard do you compare yourself to?

The first step in rethinking your life goals is to define what success means to you. Then you can make your goals to obtain it. I like this definition: "When you understand success as a state of mind, *not just an outcome,* any moment can be a victory" (*Oprah* magazine, September 2001). For some women, having a baby with Down syndrome would never be considered a success. But mothers who have these babies often say that this child revolution-ized their families, their love, and their hearts: this birth became a success for them. As we grow older, our definition of success tends to change. When I was in my early twenties, success meant having a job that paid great, having a great car, and just having all the "right stuff." Now I define success as raising confident, godly, secure daughters; loving whatever work God gives me to do; walking with God every day with joy, peace, and contentment; and having healthy, deepening relationships with my loved ones.

What does God say about success? Well, in the book of Joshua, God came to Joshua after Moses died and told him to lead the people of Israel across the Jordan River and take possession of the Promised Land. God also gave Joshua words of advice and encouragement, including His definition of success: "This book of the law shall not depart from your mouth, but you shall meditate on it day and night, so that you may be careful to do according to all that is written in it; for then you will make your way prosperous, and *then you will have success*" (Joshua 1:8; italics mine).

Moms, as we begin to set our goals, let's use God's Word as our standard, our foundation. God promises us that as we meditate on His word and follow its precepts, we will have success; and it will be God's success, not the world's! The One who made you will personalize your success! How wonderful is that?

I know some of you have become discouraged, tired, and depressed. You might have lost your sense of self so long ago that you no longer have any "get up and go," much less any hope of ever finding "you" again. If this sounds like you, I want to encourage you. At times, I too have felt so lost and depressed that I never thought I would ever get out of bed again. I didn't think I would ever be able to begin a new life. But I broke through the barrier, and you can too.

Remember the four-minute-mile barrier? Experts said that no one would ever be able to run a mile in less than four minutes. Then in 1954 a young medical student named Roger Bannister did the impossible and broke through the barrier. Today, every world-class runner can run a mile in less than four minutes, all because one person broke through the barrier. Moms, as you try to find out who you are, what you are supposed to do in this life, and how you are to go about doing it, remember that our God is the God of the Impossible. That is our hope. No one was ever supposed to live after dying; it was impossible. But one man broke the barrier of death—Jesus Christ. Since God was able to raise Jesus from the dead, He can do the impossible in your life too! Once you believe that God is going to pull you through your circumstances, you will begin to enjoy success—His success.

*There is a direct relationship between how clearly you can see your goal in your mind and how rapidly it manifests in your life.*

—*Living* magazine, August 2004

 ## Personal Inventory

Take a look at your personal life. What is your general attitude toward life? What habits do you want to change? Where do you want to be in one month, one year, five years? One of the habits of highly successful people is that of *regular goal setting.* Goals compel us to work with discipline and concentration, rather than going about our work mindlessly. Goal setting is a discipline that helps us focus. It also moves us from being reactive to being proactive about our lives.

1. What hobbies and interests did you enjoy before you had children? List these below, and put a check mark next to those you still do and an "X" next to those you want to begin doing again.

   ❏ _____    ❏ _____

   ❏ _____    ❏ _____

2. When you were a child, what did you want to be when you grew up? Has that idea changed? If so, how has it changed?

———————————————————————————

———————————————————————————

3. Make a list of all the people you know who might be resources to help you acquire your next job, and explain how they could help you.

———————————————————————————

———————————————————————————

———————————————————————————

———————————————————————————

4. Who do you know that has a healthy sense of her self? What is it about this person that you admire?

———————————————————————————

———————————————————————————

5. How would you describe what it means to be a good friend?

———————————————————————————

———————————————————————————

6. What are you living for? What are you striving toward?

———————————————————————————

———————————————————————————

7. How will you know whether or not you have been "successful" in your life?

———————————————————————————

———————————————————————————

8. Name three areas of your life where you want to recover your sense of identity and self. Then number these in order of priority.

#____ _____

#____ _____

#____ _____

---

*When we do the best we can, we never know what miracle is wrought in our life, or in the life of another.*

—Helen Keller

---

 *Everybody Wins!*

My own experience has taught me that when I don't take the time to set personal goals and then follow through with them, I feel stuck and unproductive; and my children get stuck with me. Moms, don't let yourself stay stuck! Rediscover your self by organizing your thinking and personal goals, so that you can become who God created you to be. And as you begin to change for the better, your children will see the difference and become motivated by your positive example. Everybody wins! Make Philippians 3:14 the motto you repeat to yourself each day: "I press on toward the goal to win the prize for which God has called me."

# *What I've Learned*

I bet some of you moms could write a long story about what you have learned on your journey to recover a sense of your self. As for me, the trials and hardships of adulthood caused me to sink so low that I could only look up. In this section I'd like to share some of what I have learned about work and trust, friendship, loss and recovery, and the seasons of life.

*Work and trust.* Some of you may be thinking, "No, I don't like my job, but I'm happy to have one!" Well, I am right there with you. When I had to find a job after becoming single again, my primary goal was to find something that paid decent money and allowed me to be home with my younger daughter in the mornings and afternoons. So I prayed. And then I prayed some more. I could not find anything. I kept "reminding" the Lord that time was of the essence, and I kept praying and looking. And finally I found my job! At first, I was in heaven. But then, when work became more difficult and routine, I thought I would never be able to keep doing it. Ladies, when we completely give over our situations to God, He makes it work out for us. I stopped complaining and continued to "give thanks in all things," I began to see ways to work smarter and quicker, and now I really love work! Never give up—just give the situation up to God.

*Friendship.* Public speaking and having to move from time to time have given me the opportunity to make new friends all over the country. I've met many of you just through e-mail. What fun it is to talk with other women and make new friends. But I also don't want to lose my friendships that I've had so long that they are truly golden. I have friends from elementary school that I still keep in touch with, and I try not to miss high-school reunions. I am blessed to have friends in Atlanta, Georgia (my hometown); Zionsville, Indiana; Littleton, Colorado; and now Frisco, Texas.

I try to take time to send birthday cards, e-mails, and Christmas cards, and to make phone calls. Yes, it is time consuming, but I have to keep up with my precious friends and show them I love them. I believe one of our greatest needs as moms is that of having authentic friendships with other women.

*Loss and recovery.* When I was a child, I never realized that life is full of small and great disappointments. I remember being shocked the first time bad things happened in my life. Some losses ended up working in my favor, and some I could only learn from and then move on. It helped me to understand that life works this way; then *I* could work.

It's amazing how often survivors of loss and disappointment say they eventually ended up where they needed to be. It took counseling and a lot of time before I was able to understand how to cope with big disappointments, such as the failure of my marriage, and continue with my life. One thing I did was to keep a journal; the process of writing helped me heal. I also started keeping a "gratitude journal" where I would write down five things I was thankful for each day, because when I have a thankful heart, I think less about my pain and troubles and more about the Lord. I try also to find something to laugh about each day, because it makes me feel so good.

*The seasons of life.* At this point in my life my older daughter has just graduated from college and my younger daughter is now in the eleventh grade, driving, and seemingly out of the house more than in it. I'm not very happy about any of this. It took me years to get used to "these people" living in my house and now that I've adjusted, they're gone! Seriously, I don't do well with change. It takes me an incredibly long time to work through and accept change in my life and the grief that comes with it. Why didn't anyone inform me that one day my life, my home, and my identity would change as my children grew into adulthood and I became older? Maybe subconsciously I knew all this would happen, but when it actually *did* I just wasn't ready. I'd heard of the "empty-nest syndrome" all of my life, but until it actually happened to me, I had no idea I would feel such sadness.

But as I grow older, I do see a pattern to it all. We begin life as dependent babies and young children. Then we become adolescents who need our parents yet want our own way. When we become teenagers who know everything, we *really* want our own way. Then we leave home for college or work. And as we begin to live "life," we come to realize how much we don't know and that we need our parents after all, or at least their wisdom, presence, and support.

Here are some seasons I have gone through, and some I sense are in my future:

1. *The young woman.* I look back at myself as a young teen and see such an innocent, carefree person. The most important things in life are who my friends are, buying great clothes, having boyfriends, being active in school, and dreaming about my future.

2. *The college student/employee.* Finally, the freedom I've always wanted! A future to plan for, classes to take, resumes to write, and jobs to find. The world is at my feet! Nothing seems impossible!

3. *The new bride.* What possibilities lie ahead for us! Time to build a home, a family, a future. Work hard, and then harder. Become successful.

4. *The mother of one, and then more babies.* I am a mom. Now I really need to grow up! The constant work feels overwhelming at first. I realize for the first time that I will be emotionally tied to these children for the rest of my life.

5. *The wife and mother of older children.* Life is becoming more difficult. The routine is the same each day. When will I ever feel like I have accomplished something in a day? Why do the bills continue to add up? When was the

last time my husband and I just had fun? I'm beginning to feel the pain and grief that comes from loss: Am I losing my identity? My marriage? My purpose?

6. *The middle-aged wife and mother.* When did I lose control over the kids, the house, and activities? Is it already time for my daughter to graduate from college? Why do they think they know how to run their own lives? If they aren't in my life, what is my life?

7. *The mother with an empty nest.* I wake up one day with a kick-in-the-guts question: Who am I now? Did I accomplish those dreams I used to have? Am I disappointed, or filled with peace? The world seems to be shrinking. Perhaps it's time to focus on my small achievements rather than my many failures. Did I do right by my children, by my husband, by my "neighbor," by my God?

8. *The woman nearing the end of life.* I finally see how everything really does work together for good for all those who love God and are called according to His purpose (Romans 8:28). The prodigal child returns. Disease comes and is stopped, for now. The one we loved is gone, but new love is found in the face of a child. Friends who forsake us are replaced by friends who stick by us. We finally do believe in the One who will never leave us or forsake us: this is the perfect truth I've been searching for all along. I finally come to understand that with each loss we feel grief, but in the end the grief transforms us into the image of the One who has so carefully led us. I accept the limits of my life. I welcome each new day as a gift. I finally recover a sense of my self, and find my identity.

 *Try This . . .*

As you read over these tips for recovering a sense of your self, you might think of some of your own ideas. There is space at the end of the section for you to write down ideas that come to you. Use this page as an easy reference to review, writing down results and any new tips you can think of in the spaces at the end.

*Tips for Keeping Friendships Alive:*

☀ Set aside at least one hour per week in your schedule to be with your friends. If you can add more time than that, great, but start somewhere. You might spend this hour walking with a friend once a day, going out to lunch, or making a phone call.

☀ Cultivate new friendships by joining a MOPS (Mothers of Preschoolers) group; a Sunday school class or women's Bible study; a craft, hobby, or sports group; or start a group for your neighborhood.

☀ Organize a group of your friends into a Birthday Group. It's best to have twelve friends (one for each month), but any size will work. Every month, have lunch together at a restaurant or in one of your homes to celebrate the birthday woman of that month. Collect $5 from each person for the birthday gifts (do this at the first organizational meeting). The woman whose birthday was the previous month buys one nice gift for the woman whose birthday is the next month. The person who has a birthday after the current month plans the place, time, cake, etc. This way, no one person has to do all the planning or buy all the gifts. It is so much fun!

❋ Write down a list of your dearest friends. Keep this list close by your telephone. This list will serve as a reminder in your busy life to pray for each of your friends, as well as to keep in touch with them. By setting them apart on paper, you will naturally set apart time and energy for these special friends.

❋ Now write down your own ideas for recovering your sense of self.

_____

_____

_____

*Steps for Creating Long-Term Goals:*

1. *Focus.* There are five aspects of life that require setting a goal: spiritual, financial, career, social, physical. Pick one aspect, work on it, and then move on to another until you have set long-term (five to ten years) goals for all five fundamental aspects of your life.

2. *Daydream.* Yes, kick back and daydream about what you would like to achieve with respect to the five aspects of your life, and then create a list of your dreams. Don't edit or judge what you've written. These are long-term goals you're creating, such as, "Who will I be in five years, when my children leave the nest?"

3. *Prioritize.* You probably have a long list of things you would like to accomplish, so you need to set priorities. No one really knows your situation and aspirations as well as you do, so don't compare your list with that of anyone else, or think your goals are silly. They aren't! Now, select those things on your list that are most important to you.

4. *Specify.* Turn your daydreams into specific, achievable goals. Perhaps one of your daydreams is to be a teacher. Right now you have two little babies, but you still have this dream. So write down what type of teacher you would like to become, the education you will need, what age group you wish to teach, etc.

5. *Refine.* Once you have created specific goals, take a moment to examine them. See how they measure up when compared to the following questions. If they meet the criteria below, they are good goals. If not, rewrite them.

   ❁ Do these goals specify exactly what I want to accomplish?

   ❁ Are these goals realistic? Your goals should be a stretch and require you to work hard to accomplish them, but they should not be so overly optimistic that you have no real chance of achieving them.

   ❁ Are your goals measurable? How will you know when you have reached them? For example, if your goal is something general, such as "to help children," how will you know when you've accomplished this? You can make your goals measurable by being more specific. A goal "to help children" is too general. But if your goal is to become a first-grade teacher with an emphasis on all children becoming proficient at reading, you will know when this goal is reached.

   ❁ Do these goals have a specific time frame for completing them? Every goal should have a deadline for completion. That gives it power. Make sure you specify the date when each goal is to be accomplished. I had a deadline for finishing this book, and I will bear witness that it kept me moving!

   ❁ Are these goals worthwhile? You can spend years of your life working to achieve goals that, upon later reflection, were not worth it. Don't let that happen to you. Consider whether or not a goal is worthwhile before you commit yourself to it. Have you prayed about this goal? Is it part of the plan you have sensed is God's will for you?

*Tips for Recovering from Disappointment or Loss:*

- Take care of yourself as you go through the stages of grieving by surrounding yourself with loving family and good friends.

- Go easy on yourself. Self-blame is not helpful. Admitting your own lack of control over events can help you recover more quickly.

- Count your blessings. Find something to be grateful for each day, and write it down.

- Enjoy the little things in life each day. These are the things that make life special. I used to so love to sit down with my girls after school and share a snack with them. It seems like such a little thing, but that was my favorite time of the day.

- Remember that disappointments can compel you to reinvent your life: "When one door closes, another door opens," wrote Helen Keller. The key to recovering from disappointment and loss is to develop a new set of expectations.

- Laugh! Disappointments are crummy. But when we truly realize that we are here on earth for just a quick second and the rest of our existence will be spent in eternity, then we can sit back and enjoy the ride, bumps and all.

# Set a Good Example

Setting a good example for your children can be difficult when it comes to self-development. I know that when I was depressed, I had a hard time accomplishing even the basic necessities of life. But I was conscious of the fact that in everything I did—whether good or bad—I was setting an example for my girls. Small acts of faithfulness in caring for yourself can have lasting influence on your children. So I set small daily goals: I got up every morning and made breakfast and a sack lunch for my daughters; I tried to get dressed every day (which can make a huge difference in our outlook); and I kept up with my friendships and activities (even when I didn't want to). Seeing my determination to continue living life helped my girls learn to never quit, whether it be completing college, working at a new job, or being in a marriage.

# Stress Busters!

Reducing stress really is a fabulous way to recover our true self. Moms, we all need breaks from the demands of motherhood. Here are some stress busters to help you recover a sense of your self:

- Laugh at yourself, your kids, and life. Try not to make everything such a big deal. If someone spills the milk, it really isn't the end of the world but only a little spilled milk.

- Life doesn't have to be perfect! Always do your best, but don't strive for perfection. Ease up on your children too, and you will have a much less stressful household.

- The less stuff and clutter you have, the less stress there will be in your life. Pick a room, grab a trash bag and some empty boxes, and pack up, give away, or throw away that stuff and clutter you will never miss.

- If there is a chore you hate to do, set a timer for fifteen minutes and focus on that one chore until the timer goes off. (We can do almost anything for fifteen minutes, right?)

- Organize your mornings the night before by laying out clothes, packing lunches and book bags, briefcase, etc. This greatly reduces stress in the morning.

- Walk away from your stress for a few minutes. Better yet, go outside, breathe in the fresh air, and take a short walk to regain perspective.

- Take a deep breath and hold it for a few seconds. Then slowly exhale to the count of six. Do this five times in a row and feel the tension ease.

- Then there is the classic stress buster, and my personal favorite: take a nap.

 *Bringing It Home*

When a woman gives birth, the person she used to be changes. She is now the primary caregiver, provider, and teacher of a defenseless new child. The stress that comes with this new role, especially when combined with other existing responsibilities, can be such a huge and overwhelming task that at times a new mother might have a difficult time remembering who she is at the core of her being. This chapter, hopefully, helped you rethink and restructure your current life, as well as set goals for the future. When we are organized in our personal sense of self, we feel and do well, our lives take on exciting shape, and we become more successful mothers.

The main points we have covered in this chapter on recovering your sense of self and identity are as follows:

- ☀ We moms can lose our identity when we give to everyone else and not to ourselves.

- ☀ We need to take the time to rediscover who and where we are with regard to the five aspects of life.

- ☀ When we redefine our dreams, set goals, and take time for ourselves, we become better moms.

When we work on recovering and maintaining a healthy sense of our own identity, we reap many benefits. We become stronger emotionally and are better able to withstand adversity; and our children follow our example, becoming healthier and making better choices in their own lives. Our health and sense of physical well-being improve, which greatly enhances our outlook on life. And most of all, we are better able to know and serve the Lord, and minister to others.

*I've looked a lot at what makes people successful. And I've never yet seen a real, big-time successful person who was a lone wolf. Every successful person I've known has had a nucleus of people around them who shared their passions, supported their best interests, upheld all the things that were important to them, and wanted them to succeed.*

—Dr. Phil McGraw

 *Plan of Action*

Our eighth step to becoming a more organized mom has focused on the need to "Recover Your Sense of Self." I hope this chapter on how to recover your sense of self has given you lots of food for thought, as well as tons of new ideas to try. I also hope that you are now inspired to create a plan of action for your life. What changes do you want to make as you begin to restore your sense of self, with God's help? Look back at your response to Question #8 in the "Personal Inventory" section for this chapter. Do you still agree with what you wrote and the order of importance you gave your three ideas? If you do, then complete the sentence below by writing in your #1 choice. Or, create a new #1 choice based on all you've learned in this chapter.

With God's help I want to _____.

I think I will have to change _____ in order to make this happen. I'm ready to step out in faith with God and make this change so that I can recover my sense of who God has made me to be.

One last question: What do you want written on your tombstone?

_____

_____

_____

# Step 9
# Restore Your Body

**"Therefore, I urge you . . . in view of God's
mercy, to offer your bodies as living
sacrifices, holy and pleasing to God—this is
your spiritual act of worship."
—Romans 12:1**

After giving birth to my first child, I remember waking up
each morning and thinking, "When can I go back to bed?" I was
so tired—bone tired; not-even-able-to-see tired. I was the most
fatigued and exhausted I have ever been during that first year of
motherhood. While some of you (thankfully!) won't be able to
relate to my experience, many of you completely understand the
feeling of being so tired you feel as if you've been hit by a Mack
truck! But because we are moms, we have to keep going. Just like
the Energizer Bunny, we keep going and going . . . whether we feel
like it or not. We are the glue that holds our family together.

How can you find the physical strength to keep going, to do
all you do day after day? The purpose of this chapter is to help you
find the energy to keep going. To do that, you need to concentrate
on your physical health. Some of you may be wondering how you
will find the time or energy to work on the area we'll be covering

here. You already face overwhelming challenges that cause you to feel depressed or sick from stress. Please, don't get discouraged. I've been right where you are. Help is just around the corner. Get ready to feel good again!

*Eat for health and strength.* God says in His Word that we are to take good care of our bodies. Why? Because when we commit our lives to God, His Holy Spirit takes up residence in our bodies. We have the awesome responsibility of keeping His temple clean and undefiled: "Don't you know that you yourselves are God's temple and that God's Spirit lives in you?" (1 Corinthians 3:16), Paul asks. And later in his letter to the Corinthian believers Paul reminds us that our bodies are the temple of the Holy Spirit, who lives within us, whom we have from God; therefore we are not our own: "for you have been bought with a price: therefore glorify God in your body" (1 Corinthians 6:19–20 NASB). That last phrase is what you and I are to try to do every day. In the way we conduct ourselves publicly and privately, in the things we say, the way we dress, the food we eat, and the way we care for ourselves, we reflect the God who dwells within us so that He is glorified, or not.

It is extremely hard to change old habits, especially when it comes to eating. I have to *choose* to do right by my body every single day. Remembering that what you do with your body can be a form of worship to God and a ministry to others may just be the motivation you need to make this change. God bless you as you read this chapter and consider changes that will restore your body.

Did you know that, in America, eleven million people struggle with an eating disorder, and that thirty-four million of us compulsively overeat? There is a lot of unhealthy eating going on in this country! It doesn't help that the average model we see in magazines and on television is 5'8" tall, weighs only about 100 pounds, and wears a size 2, while the average American woman is 5'4", weighs 144 pounds, and wears a size 12. Yes, something is wrong. We are being compared daily with women from outer space and we aren't going to take it anymore—so we eat!

Seriously, we all have to gain control over our eating. But if you think you might have an eating disorder, please get some help. Unhealed wounds and unhealthy habits from our past can lead to eating disorders, such as addiction to dieting, poor body image, low self-esteem or self-respect, changes in a relationship or job, or a history of eating disorders. The rest of us need to look at each day as a brand-new day. If you lost the battle yesterday, confess it to the Lord, ask for His help today, and move on! Remember, discouragement and depression are never from God, so they must be from the Enemy. Don't give in to those lies! "Greater is He who is in you than he who is in the world" (1 John 4:4 NASB).

One of the keys to successful weight loss is what Dr. Phil McGraw calls "healing your feelings."

> *If you're overweight, you're using food for other than nutritional purposes. You're not feeding your body; you're feeding your need. When you are medicating yourself with food, it's the same thing as being upset about your relationship and taking a Valium. When the Valium wears off, you still have a relationship problem. You've got to get real about what got you so bugged.*
>
> *Does everybody get stressed and anxious and depressed and lonely? Yes. Do most people turn to food when they do? Yes. Are there things you can do or turn to, other than food, that will be just as effective over the short term? Sure. Exercise, breathing, prayer, meditation, journaling. But most people go, "Eh, gimme a cupcake."*

Moms, eating the cupcake is the easy way out. It's time to plan a new lifestyle for yourself. I'll be giving you some tips on how to go about this later in the chapter.

*Exercise for health and strength.* When it comes to fitness, each one of us needs to find our own path and sense of balance. Easy, low-key workouts can keep you flexible, but they may not help you achieve your desired weight or appearance. More rigorous weight loss and muscle-building programs can slim you down and improve your general fitness, but they may not be right for you if your goal is to play competitive sports or do triathlons. Regardless of your goal, true health and fitness depend on your willingness to embrace some kind of exercise for the long haul. You'll derive far more benefit from a lifetime of moderate walking than a week of grueling training that you hate so much you burn out and quit. So what is most important to you right now? What do you want to achieve, and how hard are you willing to work at it?

Moms, say "Adios!" to a sedentary lifestyle and start moving your body. Create a program in your life that increases your rate of respiration and causes your body to become more efficient in burning fat. You might try more exercise, stretching, yoga or pilates, swimming, sports, or simply walking. I'm a big fan of walking because it's free and easy. It can be used as a quiet, soul-searching time or as a way of building relationships. Researchers at Duke University report that walking can help us lose weight: "Most adults can easily prevent weight gain by walking," says study coauthor Cris Slentz. Dr. James O. Hill, cofounder of America on the Move (*www.americaonthemove.org*) and Director of the Center for Nutrition at the University of Colorado Health Sciences Center, goes a step further:

> *By walking an extra 2,000 steps each day— about one mile— you can burn an extra 100 calories. If you combine the added activity with eliminating 100 calories each day—maybe by leaving some food on your plate—you can prevent the one to three pounds of weight gain that most Americans experience every year.*

The U.S. Department of Health and Human Services estimates that $117 billion is spent each year on treating diseases that are rooted in obesity. Walking helps prevent heart disease, cancer, and type 2 diabetes. Walking stimulates renewal of your entire body. And walking in the great outdoors might just be the best medicine we can take for rejuvenating our minds and managing our stress.

Moms, when we are healthy and strong, we are able to be the best we can be for our families. Liberate yourself from an unhealthy body with good, regular exercise!

*Rest for health and strength.* You might be thinking, "But Lane, you just told me to start moving!" Yes, I did, and yet we need to balance exercise with rest in order to stay healthy and strong. Knowing when to rest is just as important as knowing when to exercise.

God created rest. In Genesis 2:2–3 it is written that "by the seventh day God had finished the work he had been doing; so on the seventh day he rested from all his work. And God blessed the seventh day and made it holy, because on it he rested from all the work of creating that he had done." Later, in the book of Exodus, God *commands* us to rest: "Remember the Sabbath day by keeping it holy. Six days you shall labor and do all your work, but the seventh day is a Sabbath to the LORD your God. On it you shall not do any work . . . For in six days the LORD made the heavens and the earth, the sea, and all that is in them, but he rested on the seventh day. Therefore the LORD blessed the Sabbath day and made it holy" (Exodus 20:8–11).

Now that we understand that God wants us to rest and it is good for us, how do we go about doing it? Those of you moms who have tiny babies are probably up during the night (as well as those of you who have teenagers, waiting on them to come home some nights). So in general the answer is to rest whenever you can get it! I have a planned naptime every Sunday afternoon following lunch. If it's an exceptionally beautiful day, I might skip my nap, but Sunday afternoon is when I can really rest my body and prepare for a new week. Perhaps when your children come home from school, you could put your feet up as you snack with them. Or maybe you could find some rest on your job by taking a break from your desk, or even taking a five-minute power nap at your desk. One day, I was tired at work and not feeling well, so I went to my car to lie down during lunch. It was great! You have to have the intention to take short rests, along with getting at least seven hours of sleep every night. You moms who are nursing, try to rest when the baby sleeps, whenever possible.

*Pamper yourself for health and strength.* Let's look at your personal care habits. (There never really is enough time each day to do this right, is there?) Some nights I'm so worn out I just want to go to bed with my clothes on! But even if you don't think you have time for yourself, *take* time for yourself. The house is clean enough and the clothes can get washed tomorrow. Today it is time to plan your own personal care.

First, plan a time each day when you take your bath or shower. Having a regular bath time really helps ensure that you get to brush your teeth, paint your nails, shave, do all the "little things." Then, make a list of any personal products you need to buy and get them all in one trip to the discount store. What a time saver! Now it's time to throw out all the outdated prescription medications, old shampoos, broken hair clips, etc., from the bathroom. Find a place for each personal care item you buy. And don't forget to go through your closet twice a year, pulling out clothes that need to be given away, those that need to be dry cleaned, and still others that need to be stored in an out-of-season area. Also, look over your shoes, wipe down shelves, and buy hangers and hooks. Organizing your bathroom, personal items, and closet will make you feel like a new woman!

*Be careful about reading health books.*
*You may die of a misprint.*

—Mark Twain

 *Personal Inventory*

Now is a good time to review how you are doing at taking care of yourself. But don't get nervous! All of us need to take a personal inventory of ourselves in this area of our lives. Record here what you are doing for exercise, eating, rest, and personal care.

1. How would you describe your overall physical health? Check one and explain your answer.

   ❏ Poor     Explain:_____

   ❏ Fair      Explain:_____

   ❏ Great    Explain:_____

2. If you could change a few things about your body, what would they be?

   _____

3. What would you like your exercise goal to be for the next three months?

   _____

4. What are some activities that feel especially restful to you?

   _____

5. How do you pamper yourself? When was the last time you did this for yourself?

   _____

   _____

6. What is the biggest stumbling block that keeps you from taking care of yourself? How can you begin to overcome it?

_____

_____

7. Do you see your doctor and dentist for annual check-ups?

_____ Yes          _____ No

8. Name three ways you want to take better care of your body. Then number them in order of priority.

#____  _____

#____  _____

#____  _____

---

*We are what we repeatedly do. Excellence,*
*then, is not an act, but a habit.*

—Aristotle

---

 ## Everybody Wins!

Moms, as you become more physically fit and organized in caring for your body, you will develop the energy and stamina that's essential for your well-being. Then you can accomplish more, which will give you more time to spend with your children. Everybody wins! When we don't do this, we are more prone to sickness, depression, and lack of motivation; and our children suffer because of it. So, apply a few of these tips and you will begin to see results, and be even more motivated to keep going!

# What I've Learned

One thing I've learned is that our bodies and health certainly change as we age. I used to eat sweets all the time without any consequences. Not anymore! I also need more rest than I did when I was younger. I used to be able to stay up past midnight if I was working on a project, but I just can't do that anymore either. If I don't eat healthy food each day, take my walk, and rest, I begin to feel poorly and my attitude is not as good. You younger moms can cheat a little, but as we reach middle age, we definitely feel a difference. Just when I thought I was finally getting my act together, my body started falling apart!

I don't have a weight problem, but I do have a tone and strength problem, as well as some other health issues. I know that if I don't exercise, I'll get osteoporosis; and if I don't eat the proper foods, I won't have any strength at all. So I made a list of what I need to do to stay healthy and fit:

- Do aerobic exercise for a healthy heart and weight-bearing exercise for strong bones.

- Walk each day and lift small weights. Keep my five-pound weights at home and my three-pound weights at work out on my desk—and use them!

- Plan three small meals and two snacks each day.

- Don't skip a meal or a snack.

- Don't buy junk food or fast food.

- Drink plenty of water and take my vitamins and medicine.

- When tired, stop, rest, and pray. Close my eyes and breathe in and out slowly.

- Don't worry! God is in control and will never leave me or forsake me.

I learned about the importance of rest from personal experience. When my first baby was almost two, my husband and I took a vacation to Europe for a week. At that time I thought that working very hard and never stopping was the right way to live. Was I wrong! European lifestyle includes time to pause and take time for tea. I enjoyed this custom so much that when I came back home, I changed my lifestyle. Almost every afternoon since then, I stop and have some tea or coffee and a small snack. I put my feet up, go through the mail, or talk with my children when they come in from school. In fact, I schedule this time to coincide with the time they come home, and it's a great time to have snacks together and talk about the day. I know you working moms can't do this at home, but take a break at work every day. It will make you feel healthier and stronger.

Also, whether my children were tired or not, every Sunday after church and lunch we would have a "reading/rest time." Since this had been the custom from the time they were very young, they never complained. They could sleep or read. But momma was for sure going to nap! This rest time rejuvenated me for the rest of the week.

When we are single, there seems to be plenty of time for everything, especially our personal care. So when our babies are born, we have to work harder to keep these habits up. I have learned to keep my personal care on a schedule and move fast! I usually bathe at night so I can have more time in the mornings. I keep my medicines and vitamins, hair supplies, and makeup, in the same place so I can find everything I need quickly. I work at keeping my closet organized so I can locate my clothes, shoes, etc. Believe me, there have been times when I have been in such a hurry that my clothes ended up in a heap. But I found that if I can keep everything organized, I spend less time washing clothes, looking for lost items, and getting stressed when trying to get dressed for the day. I also try to use just a few items, instead of buying every type of makeup or hair product on the market. Keeping it simple really does help!

 *Try This . . .*

Moms, remember that one of the main reasons you are working on your health is because your body is God's temple, and we are to reflect His presence within us to a suffering world. Remember also that self-control is one of the fruits of the Holy Spirit (Galatians 5:23). Our children learn by what they see us doing, so we need to be the best example possible for them to follow, and this for the sake of their well-being now and in the future.

*Tips on What, When, and How to Eat Each Day:*

- Have a goal. Know what it is that you want for your body and go after it.

- Plan to succeed. Write down everything you want to achieve and how you will do it.

- Plan what you eat. Sign up to be a member of a group like Weight Watchers or Jenny Craig, or get a book that someone from your local health food store recommends.

- Take it one step at a time. You may be changing habits and a lifestyle that has been with you for years.

- Know your "danger zone." Mine is late at night. If I don't go to bed at a decent, hour I start getting hungry, and the next thing I know I'm eating chunky peanut butter and chocolate morsels with chocolate milk! So I try to go to bed on time . . . and stay away from the kitchen.

- Don't rely on willpower. We are all human, and we cannot be in control all of the time. So stick to your plan, respect your danger zones, and keep healthy foods in your home.

- Use common sense. Eat less than you used to and move your body more. Don't let food be the focus of your life by measuring every morsel.

- Don't skip breakfast. There is a 420% chance that you will gain weight if you don't eat breakfast! If you don't have time to eat, have a protein drink.

- Eat four to five times a day. Besides three small meals, eat a light morning and afternoon snack that consists of foods such as fruit, yogurt, cheese, or wheat crackers. Do not eat anything after dinner. (If you adhere to this rule, you *will* lose weight!)

- Be smart about carbs. Not all carbohydrates are the same. Carbs with a low glycemic index—such as fruits, nuts, vegetables, whole-grain breads, and legumes—break down more slowly and don't convert as easily to fat. You need these in your diet.

- Avoid refined sugars, white flour, processed foods, and corn syrup. Corn syrup, one of the leading causes of obesity, is found in soft drinks and sweetened juices.

- Eat what you enjoy, in moderation. Eat part of the chocolate bar and save the rest for another day. Buy low-fat ice cream and enjoy every bite.

- Focus on how you look, not on the weight scales. If your clothes begin to feel tight, cut back on what you eat. A little bit of change each day will make a huge difference.

- Be in charge of your food. Don't let food be in charge of you. Set boundaries as to what is appropriate and what isn't.

*Tips for Health and Longevity:*

- Get at least thirty minutes of moderate exercise every day.

- Choose exercise you enjoy, possibly a form of exercise you can do with someone you enjoy being with.

- Monitor your weight.

- Increase your fitness gradually. This yields even more benefits.

*"Breaking into a sweat regularly is a crucial part of becoming and staying a healthy person," says Dr. Ralph Brovard, a sports medicine specialist at Regions Hospital in St. Paul, Minnesota "People forget exercise is medicine. Daily exercise is perhaps the most powerful tool you can prescribe for yourself; a variety of regular activity helps prevent cardiovascular disease, type 2 diabetes, osteoporosis, arthritis and just about every other affliction that strikes us as we age."*

—Experience Life, *December 2005*

*Tips for Weight Loss:*

- ✸ Set realistic short- and long-term goals for weight loss.

- ✸ Get moderate to intense cardiovascular exercise four to six times per week, to create a caloric deficit.

- ✸ Aim for thirty minutes of higher-intensity circuit or interval training for two to three of your cardio sessions.

- ✸ Weight train two to three times per week, focusing on compound joint exercises. Use enough weight to near failure at ten to twelve reps.

*Tips for Performance:*

- ✸ Set performance-based goals.

- ✸ Design and organize your workouts according to a solid workout/recovery schedule.

- ✸ Make nutrition a priority, regardless of whether you are watching your weight.

- ✸ Be sure to get enough omega-3 essential fatty acids and antioxidants through diet and supplements.

- ✸ Cross-train to avoid injury (e.g., walk one day, bike the next).

⚛ Get enough rest to help your body repair damage and rebuild energy stores.

—adapted from *Experience Life* magazine, March 2003

*Tips to Help You Rest:*

⚛ If you don't have time to rest during the day, breathe! When you are at a stoplight, in the carpool lane, or waiting in line, take a deep breath and count to six. Then, very slowly let the air out, also counting to six. Do this for one minute. You will be amazed how much better you feel! If you can close your eyes while doing this breathing exercise, even better.

⚛ Find ten minutes during the day when you can just sit and be still.

⚛ If you have children under the age of four, nap when they nap (don't catch up on housework!), especially if your babies are still waking you up at night.

⚛ If you work outside the home, try napping on the weekends.

⚛ For those of you with babies and toddlers, try giving yourself "time-outs" during the day or when your husband comes home. Tell him you need a "time out" . . . in the bathtub or outside for a walk.

⚛ Schedule time for sleep. We have so many 24/7 stores, computers, and television that keep us up! Just as we have to discipline ourselves to eat and exercise, we must discipline ourselves to sleep.

⚛ Embrace the day by waking up with thoughts of blessings and gratitude for the Lord and the life He has given you. Welcome each new day!

⚛ Start and end each day by reading God's Word or an encouraging book, by journaling, and/or by praying.

I was watching Dr. Phil recently (I'm sure it was research for this book), and he said, "A mother at home with children is actually working two full-time jobs. And if she also has a 'job,' then it's three full-time jobs." Moms, I pray that your husband, mother, or family members are there to help and support you. But if not, my prayer is that you will find the strength in the Lord to be the best that you can be. Keeping your body healthy is a great start! When you feel good, you can achieve so much more in life. I hope you latch on to some of the tips above to help you meet your goal to restore your body.

# Set a Good Example

What we do (and don't do) can be valuable examples for our children. Along with modeling good, healthy habits, such as exercising, eating properly, resting, and personal care, the way we interact with others is extremely important. The way we relate to others in our marriage and extended families, as well as the poor and needy, and our friendships, becomes an example of behavior our children will follow as they grow and mature.

Think about some examples you may be setting for your children right now. One of the most important examples you can set is the way you relate to your husband. For you single moms, your dating relationships and the respect you show yourself is very important. One way to show your children how important your marriage and your husband are to you is to take a weekend get-away twice a year. Your husband is your first priority, not your children. He is working very hard to support the family, and the stress of doing that is great. He needs to know you love him more than anyone else. Keep the fires burning! If money is an issue, have family or friends take the children and just stay home, going out for breakfast and dinner, just the two of you. Plan weekly dates also, even if you just go out for coffee. I have heard it said many times that the greatest gift we moms can give our children is to love our husbands.

When it comes to friendships, my own mother set a great example for me. She was always in contact with her friends, through monthly bridge games or dinner parties. She encouraged us to reach out to friends, to have get-togethers, and to remember their birthdays. She never forgot any of our friends' names and was always encouraging us to have them over. If I had a friend move away, get married, or have a baby, our home would be the place for the party or shower. I hope I have passed on this example to my girls. We all reap the benefits when we have good and loving relationships in our lives.

"Golly, I feel ten years younger!"

"Golly, so do I!"

© BIL KEANE, INC. KING FEATURES SYNDICATE

# Stress Busters!

Moms, stress just comes with the territory of motherhood. Since we can expect to feel it some days, what can we do to get a break from it and feel physically restored?

- ☀ Set aside one night this week and declare it "Spa Night." On Spa Night you have no responsibility whatsoever for your husband or children. You get to lock yourself in your bathroom and for several hours enjoy a luxurious bath (soothing music, candlelight, and a relaxing beverage are all highly recommended), a manicure and pedicure, and a facial. You'll feel like a million!

- ☀ Maintain a positive attitude; this can make all the difference when we are stressed.

- ☀ If you are a single mom, try to find some place (maybe your church) or some one who can watch your children for a couple of hours once a week. You need to take a break during the hard, workweek to have some adult fun. Creating a co-op, where you swap child care with other mothers you trust, is one way of providing a regular time for yourself without any expense.

- ☀ Make an appointment with yourself, just as you would a business appointment, whether it's to exercise, to cook and eat healthy food, or to rest.

- ☀ Moms of older children and teenagers might want to find a support group or parenting class that can provide tips for better parenting.

*Bringing It Home*

Restoring your body can work a miracle in your life. When we eat healthy foods, exercise our bodies, and get enough rest, our entire being changes for the better. We then have the energy and focus to organize other areas in our lives that benefit not only us but our children as well. In this chapter we have talked about the fact that:

- ☀ We take care of our bodies because they are the temple of God.

- ☀ When we are physically fit, we can do more for ourselves, our families, and others.

- ☀ Everything in your life will improve when you become the healthiest YOU God created.

Moms, when you are physically fit, you have more stamina to accomplish all you have to do. Your attitude becomes more positive because of all the endorphins released when you exercise. You become a more positive influence in the lives of your husband and children. You have the desire to eat healthier foods. And you become a great role model for your children.

## *S. M. A. R. T.*

*Smart eating*
*Move your body*
*Air to breathe and plenty of water to drink*
*Rest*
*Treat yourself well!*

 # Plan of Action

For our ninth step to becoming a more organized mom, we have focused on the need to "Restore Your Body." My prayer is that you will be motivated to do the things you need to do in order to become a vessel for the Lord.

Think about what inspires you the most: being a loving wife, a good mom, helping other people, utilizing your gifts at work. You can make those pursuits even more rewarding and meaningful (and more fun!) by doing them in the most competent, generous, and helpful way you can. Let your new energy propel you forward, and you will find yourself in some wonderful places that your old self never dreamed of going.

Now it's time to ask yourself, where do you want to be with your physical health? How do you want to get there, with God's help? Now look back at your response to Question #8 in the "Personal Inventory" section. Do you still agree with what you wrote and the order of importance you gave your three ideas? If you do, then complete the sentence below by writing in your #1 choice. Or, create a new #1 choice based on all that you've learned in this chapter.

With God's help I want to _____.

I think I will have to change _____ in order to make this happen. I'm ready to step out in faith with God and make this change so that I can restore my body to be all that God created it to be.

## A Strong Woman

*A strong woman works out every day to keep her body in shape . . . but a woman of strength builds relationships to keep her soul in shape.*

*A strong woman isn't afraid of anything . . . but a woman of strength shows courage in the midst of her fear.*

*A strong woman won't let anyone get the best of her . . . but a woman of strength gives the best of herself to everyone.*

*A strong woman makes mistakes and avoids the same in the future . . . but a woman of strength realizes life's mistakes can also be unexpected blessings, and capitalizes on them.*

*A strong woman wears a look of confidence on her face . . . but a woman of strength wears grace.*

*A strong woman has faith that she is strong enough for the journey . . . but a woman of strength has faith that it is in the journey that she will become strong.*

*—Author Unknown*

# Step 10

## Renew Your Mind

**"Do not conform any longer to the pattern
of this world, but be transformed
by the renewing of your mind."
—Romans 12:2**

On our journey to become more organized moms, we have looked at the importance of recovering a sense of our self and restoring our bodies. In this chapter we look at the need to renew our minds as well. What and how we think can make or break a successful life and family: "As a man thinks in his heart, so is he," says Proverbs 23:7 (NKJV). How we think can literally transform our reality. As we continue learning how to restore our selves, this next step focuses on our mental health. We can withstand a great deal in life if our minds are focused on the Lord and His ways. How does a person become wise? The first step is to trust and revere the Lord (Proverbs 1:8).

*Make good choices.* Moms, the most important battles in our lives are fought in our minds. Just as our bodies need healthy food in order to feel well, our minds need to be "fed" wholesome truths. Mental junk food causes the mind to become flabby, weak, and vulnerable to temptation. The saying "Put junk in, get junk out" is so true. Some examples of mental junk food include watching too much television and/or R-rated movies; books and magazines that focus on inappropriate subject matter; pornography; speaking and listening to vulgar speech, etc. If my mind is fed by the sight of things that are detrimental to who I am in the Lord, this eventually affects the way I act.

The reason advertising companies spend *millions* of dollars to promote their products is because it works—after seeing their products on commercials, billboards, and magazine covers, we really *do* start thinking we need their product. Did you know that the pornography industry, which is available to anyone at any time online, has been proven to play a significant role in the increased incidence of divorce, child molestation, domestic violence, and serial killings in America? Moms, we need to be careful about what we expose ourselves to, what our children see, and what we allow in our homes.

What we allow in our homes will be different for each family. Some think Walt Disney depictions of evil and violence are alright, since most of them are based on fairy tales, but other families are more cautious. My rule of thumb is to ask myself, what would Jesus say if He were sitting next to my child watching this show? You should get a pretty good idea of what to do when you ask that question. My personal opinion is that, even if you are with your child, he or she does not need to see R-rated movies.

Moms, controlling your thought processes can be a powerful way to stop the negative influences at work in your life. The more you understand how your thinking affects your role as a mother, the better care you can give your family. Getting your *mind* organized is essential to getting your *life* organized.

Scripture instructs us not to look to the world for the origin of our thoughts and ideas, but to God's Word, where we are renewed in our mind. Romans 12:2 says, "Do not conform any longer to the pattern of this world, but be transformed by the renewing of your mind." Take time to study what God says and ponder what He means in His Word: "Do your best to present yourself to God as one approved, a workman who does not need to be ashamed and who correctly handles the word of truth" (2 Timothy 2:15). Moms, we need to make a conscious effort and choice to turn *away from* Madison Avenue's media blitz and *look toward* the truth of Scripture, which is the only place we will ever find true life, true hope, and true joy. Remember, mental junk food causes our minds to become weak and vulnerable to temptation. Let's look at some signs that may indicate your mental diet is in need of better nutrition; signs such as anger, stress, anxiety, depression, worry, and fear.

*Control your anger.* For all of us, anger is an emotion we need to monitor. If you allow anger and bitterness to take root, the Enemy gains a foothold that can eventually destroy both you and your family. Don't let this happen to you. The book of Proverbs is chock full of verses about the destructive power of anger. And the epistle of James offers this advice: "Everyone should be quick to listen, slow to speak and slow to become angry, for man's anger does not bring about the righteous life that God desires." The writer then gives this admonition to get rid of "mind junk": "Get rid of all moral filth and the evil that is so prevalent and humbly accept the word planted in you" (James 1:19–21). Concerning the dangers of bitterness, Hebrews 12:15 speaks about being careful that "no bitter root grows up to cause trouble and defile many."

None of us wants to yell at our children, but we all get angry sometimes and yell at our kids. What can you do when the steam starts coming out of your ears and you know you're about to blow? Step away from the situation, take a huge breath, and let all your anger out with a prayer for God to help you control your temper, give you wisdom and patience, and be a good example to your children of the appropriate way to handle conflict. Self-control is the fruit of the Holy Spirit, so pick that fruit off the tree and take a bite! I know that God the Father, Son, and Holy Spirit never had four children in diapers or a teenager driving off in a huff after talking back, but Jesus did have many sisters and brothers, and I know He understands the tremendous stress you and I have to handle.

*Let go of guilt.* I heard one time about a mother who was feeling guilty that she wasn't doing for her daughter what "all the other mothers" were doing. For example, her daughter told her she was the only mom who never brought snacks for her Brownie troop or stayed to help with the meeting. So when the next Brownie meeting was scheduled, this mom rushed through her work at the office, left early, rushed across town in time to pick up a pre-ordered snack, and arrived at the meeting with a halo of motherly goodness over her head. That feeling quickly faded when the troop leader asked where her daughter was. In a flash of panic this poor mother realized she had forgotten to pick up her daughter. She forgot to bring her own child!

I know many of you can completely identify with this story. There's so much going on in our lives that, when others pile guilt on us, we just want to curl up and quit. Our own mothers and grandmothers didn't have to deal with the hectic schedule or the avalanche of parental-advice books that add guilt to what we do today. Just when you think you're doing a pretty good job as a mom, along comes an author explaining how, with just a little bit more effort *on your part,* little Johnny could be the next Superman! What many of these books presume is that parenting is a formula, like algebra, when really it is a lifelong dance between individual personalities and self-wills. They neglect to note that we moms are trying our very best, while living frazzled lives.

Here's the bottom line on guilt: "When a man's ways are pleasing to the LORD, he makes even his enemies live at peace with him" (Proverbs 16:7). There will always be people who try to make us feel guilty for this or that. So, take everything to the Lord and ask Him to let you know whether or not the criticism is valid. Then focus on living for the Lord and not to please others. Everything else will fall into place if we make serving the Lord our goal. Confess to God all those past mistakes and sins, and memorize Romans 8:1: "There is now no condemnation for those who are in Christ Jesus." When you are in Christ and He is in you, your sins are forgiven and you are set free to walk away from the heavy weight of guilt.

*Forgive yourself.* I don't know a mom who hasn't at one time or another experienced the awful feeling that she has failed her children. Everyone, including the great people of the Bible, failed at some point in their lives. Just look at the track record of some well-known Bible characters, and then recall what God did through them—in spite of their failures. Better yet, photocopy this and tape it to your mirror!

---

## People God Used Despite Their Failings

*Noah was a drunk . . .*
*Abraham was way too old . . .*
*Jacob was a liar . . .*
*Joseph was severely abused . . .*
*Gideon was afraid . . .*
*Sampson was a womanizer . . .*
*Rahab was a prostitute . . .*
*Jeremiah and Timothy were very young . . .*
*King David had an affair and was a murderer . . .*
*Moses was a murderer and couldn't speak well . . .*
*Elijah was suicidal . . .*
*Jonah ran from God . . .*
*Job went bankrupt . . .*
*John the Baptist ate bugs and lived a different life . . .*
*Peter denied Christ . . .*
*The disciples fell asleep while praying . . .*
*Martha worried about everything . . .*
*Mary Magdalene was demon-possessed . . .*
*The Samaritan woman was divorced many times and living in sin . . .*
*Zaccheus was a corrupt tax collector . . .*
*Paul was a Pharisee, hated by the Jews, and killed Christians . . .*
*but God forgave them when they repented, overlooked their failures, and used them for His glory!*

*— Author Unknown*

---

If God can use them, He can use you!

*Stress and Anxiety.* Stress and anxiety affect our thoughts and sap our strength. Of all doctor visits, 75% are due to stress-related illnesses. But there is no way around it: stress and anxiety are products of our modern way of life. What isn't there to worry about? Every night on the news we learn about wars, unemployment, the cost of living rising higher than anyone's wages, and one famous person divorcing that famous person to marry a different famous person.

Research reveals that women experience anxiety more often and more intensely than men. Perhaps that's because women assume the role of comforter and protector. As mothers, daughters, and wives we are always on the alert for signs of danger to our families. This is good for our families. But when we give to others without any limits or boundaries, then our stress level escalates out of control.

Since 1994, when the National Institute of Health mandated that both sexes be broadly represented in government-funded medical research, scientists have been discovering that women are hard-wired differently when it comes to stress: "Women report more day-to-day stress," says Prof. Alice Domar of Harvard Medical School, Director of the Mind/Body Center for Women's Health at the Boston IVF clinic and the author of *Self-Nurture.* In fact, twice as many women suffer from general anxiety disorders than men. The reasons? Women are affected by:

- ❂ *Multitasking.* The multiple roles women play—spouse, mother, home manager, employee, caregiver, and friend—and the constant juggling of the demands each role requires increase the emotional pressure they feel. In fact, recent studies have found that in women there is more interconnection between both hemispheres of the brain than in men. Women have *all* their senses engaged *all* the time. We hear the baby crying upstairs at the same time that we're making dinner, listening to our mother recount her day over the phone, and helping a child with a math equation.

❁ *Caregiving.* Two of our most outstanding qualities—nurturing others and deferring to others—often get in the way of caring for our own needs. Nearly one woman in four becomes a caregiver between the age of thirty-five and forty-four, and more than one in three (35%) between the ages of fifty-five and sixty-four.

❁ *Physical vulnerability.* Women are subject to physical threats that don't typically affect men. We also have a harder time with physical tasks than men. As active as I am, I still don't have the strength for some chores and tasks around the house. It is so frustrating not to be able to do something just because I'm not strong or tall enough.

❁ *Cultural pressures.* "In order for a woman to consider herself happy," says Domar, "she has to be in a good relationship, be happy with her kids, her friends have to like her, her job has to be going well, her house has to look really good—and she has to be thin." Our personal goals and achievements are usually measured according to what society thinks is important—and these change with the times.

❁ *Anxiety over falling short.* Many women struggle to balance work and family, and feel guilty about not doing either job well. Our society still is not designed to accommodate working women, says Domar, noting that one researcher compared the stress level of mothers to that of soldiers in combat! In fact, 85% of working moms say they felt guilty about combining work and family, compared to 0% of working dads.

❁ *Being too busy.* Motivational speaker Zig Ziegler says that being busy is like Being Under Satan's Yoke. The busier we are the more stressed we become, and this diminishes the effectiveness of what we give to our families, ourselves, and the kingdom of God. Moms, stop doing so much! Cut out the "good" things and keep only the "best" things in your life.

Some stress and anxiety can be positive, being the body's normal fight-or-flight response. When your body feels threatened, anxiety kicks in and your sense of awareness and attention is heightened. This provides the adrenaline rush you need to rise to the occasion. The response, however, is intended to be short-lived; you comfort your hurt child or turn in the report by the deadline . . . and relax.

Problems develop when you live in a constant state of alertness and the sense of anxiety cannot be relieved. Dr. Elson M. Haas, author of *Staying Healthy with the Seasons,* identifies seven types of stress:

- Physical: intense exertion, manual labor, lack of sleep, travel
- Chemical: drugs, alcohol, caffeine, nicotine, and environmental pollutants such as cleaning chemicals and pesticides
- Mental: perfectionism, worry, anxiety, long hours at work
- Emotional: anger, guilt, loneliness, sadness, fear
- Nutritional: food allergies, vitamin and mineral deficiencies
- Traumatic: injuries or burns, surgery, illness, infections, extreme temperatures
- Psycho-spiritual: troubled relationships; financial or career pressures; challenges that threaten life goals, spiritual alignment, and one's general state of happiness

I hope this list has helped you identify the source of your stress. When you look over the tips I offer below, be bold and try several of them. Most importantly, put God at the center of your life. God is the Prince of Peace and your Wonderful Counselor. When we focus on the Lord and trust that He knows how to take care of us, we can relax and enjoy life as we have entrusted it to Him. Focus on Jesus and not on your circumstances.

*Deal with depression.* Depression is a paralyzing, immobilizing feeling of darkness and despair; an engulfing loss of hope. I have suffered from it. Many of you have too. Depression puts your mind, body, and emotions into a holding pattern while it throws out the welcome mat to pessimism, low self-esteem, and apathy. Instead of adjusting to a setback and dealing with its consequences, we continue to dwell on it—week after week, month after month—until no thing and no one gives us any pleasure. When this happens, you may be what is called "clinically depressed." Chronic depression—with or without an obvious trigger—is for the most part a biological illness, just like diabetes or a heart attack. But this illness is caused by an imbalance of certain chemicals in the brain. Fortunately, like most illnesses, clinical and chronic depression almost always respond to treatment.

Roughly 17% of all Americans are affected by depression; that's around fifteen million people. Depression is a signal that there needs to be a change in your life. God can use depression to motivate us toward that change.

There are many safe and effective medications on the market that can be prescribed when we have to deal with depression caused by a chemical imbalance. Hormonal changes that come with menstrual periods, menopause, even the birth of a baby, can cause chemical imbalances in a woman's body. Postpartum depression, that hard-to-understand depression that affects new mothers, has been in the news a lot lately. Since this is a book for moms, we need to take a closer look at this type of depression.

Having a baby is supposed to be one of the happiest times in a woman's life. However, some women become overwhelmed by feelings of sadness and constant stress instead. Problems arise when the mother begins to feel guilt over these feelings and doesn't share her "baby blues" with anyone who might be able to help. The reality is that 85% of all new mothers experience these blues, with 8 to 15% suffering severe symptoms.

After a woman gives birth, her hormone levels fluctuate. Hormones such as estrogen and other chemicals, such as serotonin and dopamine (which give the body a sense of well-being), are at a low level. If they're in short supply, situations that wouldn't normally depress a woman might make her feel sad. Lack of sleep and sporadic, sometimes unhealthy eating habits can contribute to the feeling of distress. Some mothers are able to get through this phase with support and help from others. However, some mothers with extreme postpartum depression commit suicide and/or infanticide. This is a tragic situation that can be avoided if all those involved take the time to see what is really going on and seek medical help.

I urge any woman who suspects she might be suffering from depression to seek medical advice as soon as possible. You don't have to display all the symptoms of clinical depression to be considered depressed. Don't be embarrassed that your friends might find out, and don't wait until it gets worse. Depression in women outnumbers its occurrence in men by a ratio of two to one. Several reasons account for this. Women are more isolated than men. Women have less education and fewer options in life than men. Also, the presence of young children at home, especially multiple children, can cause depression to escalate if a woman has insufficient support or an unstable marital history. Women's bodies produce only half the amount of serotonin that men produce. Estrogen is a feel-good chemical, but before menstruation, after delivery of a baby, and when a woman is peri-menopausal, a woman's estrogen level drops, and this can lead to depression. So if you know someone who might be depressed, urge her to see her doctor—even offer to make the appointment for her and take her there. We who are healthy need to help those who might be drowning.

The third type of depression is the kind associated with loss. The loss can be a concrete loss, such as the death of a loved one, a divorce, severe illness—yours or a loved one's—moving, loss of one's job, financial loss, or specific relationship problems. Or, the loss can be abstract, such as feeling depressed over a lost childhood, experiencing an empty nest, becoming older, losing friendships, or feeling regret about the past. Some reasons for depression can fall into any category. Adults who were abused as children, either physically, verbally, emotionally, or sexually, might have this memory buried so deeply that they are depressed and not even sure why. If any of you moms endured such abuse, I beg you to go to a trained medical professional who can help you work through this. These hidden hurts will come out in different forms, and the cycle of abuse will be handed down through your own children if not treated.

Christian counselor H. Norman Wright wrote a book and video series entitled *Crisis Care.* In the book he writes, "If you don't recognize something as a loss, then you don't spend time and energy dealing with it and grieving over it." People experience different losses, but they all need to be identified. One mom who suffered from postpartum depression said, "I discovered I was grieving my loss of control, freedom, and former lifestyle. Realizing this allowed me to grieve consciously and continue to move forward with a healthy, hopeful mindset." Perhaps you are depressed over a loss you haven't quite identified. Pray and ask God to heal your hurts. Remember that the healthier we are in mind, body, and spirit, the better we will be as moms.

Symptoms of depression and loss include:

- A profound sense of sadness
- Feeling disconnected
- Feeling numb
- Feeling that you cannot stop crying
- Feeling hopeless, pessimistic
- Inability to enjoy favorite activities
- Sleeping too much or not enough
- Thoughts of suicide
- Restlessness and irritability
- Refusal to talk
- Experiencing flashbacks, nightmares
- Headaches

These symptoms are common and, although painful, they are part of the healing process.

One thought that might help you is that there are examples of depression throughout the Bible. Elijah suffered suicidal depression. King David wrote many of the Psalms to help heal his depression. The prophet Jeremiah expressed an overwhelming sense of loss over the destruction of Jerusalem. And Naomi, the mother-in-law of Ruth, became so depressed she changed her name. Job lost everything he had: his children, his home, his livestock, his entire fortune, and even his health. Scripture doesn't reveal whether or not he was depressed, but I believe the natural human reaction to such tragic losses certainly suggests that he was. I also believe his wife was depressed. She counseled Job to "curse God and die!" The prophet Jonah pleaded with God, "LORD, please take my life from me, for death is better to me than life" (Jonah 4:3 NASB). In all of these examples God was still present, and He helped His people endure all the feelings, emotions, and pain that accompany loss. It is important, moms, to understand that you too will undergo many trials in life. Each one of us responds differently. Some will get depressed. My prayer is that we begin to understand depression a little better, so we can learn to overcome it.

Do not feel guilty when you are depressed. We are no different from the people of the Bible. Depression can be a healing process and a chance to grow our trust in God. Depression is not a sin; it is a natural response to loss. However, sin—which is living apart from God's will—can be a cause of depression. In 1 Peter 2:11, the writer admonishes us to "abstain from sinful desires, which war against your soul." If I make choices that are sinful, there will be consequences, one of them being depression.

Is there a root of bitterness in your heart? Anger? Unforgiveness? "Get rid of all bitterness, rage and anger, brawling and slander, along with every form of malice. Be kind and compassionate to one another, forgiving each other, just as in Christ God forgave you" (Ephesians 4:31–32). Moms, forgiveness is the key to being healed of depression. Here's why:

- Forgiveness is the *antidote* for resentment and anger.
- Unforgiveness damages our health, our sense of peace, and our relationships.

Right now you may be remembering great hurts and injustices that have happened to you. But God's Word is so clear that forgiveness is THE key to a blessed life here on earth. Jesus said that "whatever you bind on earth will be bound in heaven, and whatever you loose on earth will be loosed in heaven" (Matthew 18:18).

*Forgiveness is not . . .*

- a feeling; you will not always *feel* like forgiving.
- pretending you were not hurt.
- saying that what the other person did really wasn't wrong.
- saying you must trust the other person (especially in cases of abuse).
- freeing the other person of responsibility.

*Forgiveness is . . .*

- a decision; I *choose* to forgive.
- obeying God.
- taking responsibility for my actions and attitudes.
- choosing to live God's love, joy, and peace.

The best way to heal when someone hurts you is to forgive and not seek revenge. Saying "I forgive you" (in your mind or to the person) could be the most difficult and powerful thing you'll ever do. To forgive doesn't mean to give in; it means to let go. You forgive not so much for the sake of others but for your *own* sake. In many cases the other person isn't even aware that you are holding these feelings of pain and bitterness. Forgiving will give you a greater sense of power. A rabbi who lost his family in the Holocaust said he forgave because he chose not to bring Hitler with him to America. When you forgive, you reclaim your power to choose. It doesn't matter whether someone who has wronged you deserves forgiveness: you deserve to be free.

*This is the great conversation in our life: to recognize and believe that the many unexpected events are not just disturbing interruptions of our projects, but the way in which God molds our hearts and prepares us.*

—Henri Nouwen

 *Personal Inventory*

Taking your own "inventory" is very important, because you need to really look at what is going on in your mind if you are to move forward with clarity, compassion, peace, and joy. So, take a few moments to record here the way you currently "organize" your mental health. Be honest with yourself. Remember, acknowledging the problem is the first step toward changing it.

1. Think back to your childhood and other memories from your past. Who and what (events, circumstances, etc.) might you need to forgive in order to move forward today?

   _____

   _____

   _____

2. Where do you feel "trapped" in your own thinking? Name some specific areas.

_____

_____

_____

3. What positive thoughts and memories would you like to focus on, in order to reduce your feelings of anxiety or stress?

_____

_____

_____

4. It is so easy to have self-pity and feel like a victim, but it isn't healthy or right. In the space below, write down ways that will help you focus more on your blessings and less on your past or present difficulties and losses.

_____

_____

_____

5. Name three ways you can choose to be happy.

   #1 _____

   #2 _____

   #3 _____

6. Name some people in your life that you need to stay connected with in order to stay mentally healthy.

_____

_____

_____

7. Name three aspects of your mental health that you want to begin changing. Then number them in order of priority.

#\_\_\_\_ _____

#\_\_\_\_ _____

#\_\_\_\_ _____

*It may sound trite, but today is the only time you have.*
*It's too late for yesterday. And you can't depend on tomorrow.*
*That's why today matters.*

—John C. Maxwell

 ## Everybody Wins!

Moms, I know it's hard to find motivation when you feel there is no hope for the future. If you are feeling depressed and having a hard time focusing on all you need to do, you will feel drained of all momentum. But like any discipline, your attitude will not take care of itself. You need to attend to it daily. When you make small changes in your mental health, everybody wins! You win by gaining victory over the dark times in life. Your children win by learning ways to cope with difficulty, and by seeing that life is truly good. Remember what John Wooden says: "Things turn out best for the people who make the best of the way things turn out."

*What I've Learned*

One thing I've learned about staying healthy mentally is just how important it is to live in the present. When I was young, I loved watching *Star Trek* on television. In one episode Captain Kirk met up with some space beings who had the ability to probe his mind. As they probed his mind, they asked him questions about his past, and then they took him to those places in his mind so that it seemed to him he was actually reliving those days. Kirk, however, continually flashed back to his wife's tragic death, and he became very frustrated. When he asked the aliens why they kept returning him to that memory, they replied, "Because this is where you exist." "No!" he insisted, "I'm the captain of the spaceship. That is where I exist." After repeated mind trips and frustrations, the captain finally understood. In his subconscious he really did exist in that past time. He had not moved forward, past that tragedy that happened years ago. He had to *choose* to live in the present.

I've also learned that "overdoing it" causes me stress, and stress makes me angry. Attending Bible study, working, volunteering in the community or at church, keeping my house, making meals, and raising my children are just too much! Every time I speak to a group of moms, at least one laughs and says, "I know I'm too busy, but I like everything I do!" I've learned the value of saying "No."

I have learned that having joy is a matter of choice. I can either be despondent and sad, or I can accept "my lot in life" and make the most of the life I have. Am I happy about everything that has happened in my life? No! But I choose to take the road of positive thought and action. I know that I am accountable for my happiness, and I refuse to be a victim. My well-being lies deep within my subconscious mind. If my focus is on the past, then I can't operate in the present. I have to ask myself, where is my focus? Not beat myself up for making mistakes! I have to give my hurts over to

the Lord, let Him carry these burdens, and then walk in the new-
ness of each new day.

I have learned that people don't drown by falling in the
water; they drown by staying there. Don't let yourself drown, dear
sister. Get out of the water, dry yourself off, and move to dry land!

 *Try This...*

Here are some tips that can help you get on track mentally.
Write the ones that strike a chord on a 3 x 5 index card, so you can
look at them throughout the day and remember to implement
them.

❋ *Pay attention to what you think about.* If you seem to get
stuck in negative thoughts or situations where you have
no control, break that habit by pondering what is good in
your life and in God's Word.

❋ *Instead of worrying, pray.* Only God can change what we
cannot change and what we have no control over: "Do not
be anxious about anything, but in everything, by prayer
and petition, with thanksgiving, present your requests to
God. And the peace of God, which transcends all understanding, will guard your hearts and your minds in Christ
Jesus" (Philippians 4:6–7).

❋ *Live in the present.* The past is over, done with, gone.
Learn from it and the mistakes you made, so that you can
show up for today.

❋ *Take responsibility for your actions.* Avoiding responsibility
for our actions is the single most effective way to get stuck
or stay stuck in a life that won't work for you, or anyone
else in your life.

- *Don't procrastinate.* Procrastination brings no joy, satisfaction, or relief. It's an indulgence that hurts families, careers, and children. If you need to do something, get started. Once you begin, the feeling of relief will help you complete the task. Organization is the best antidote to procrastination.

- *Stay connected to others.* Sharing your thoughts, feelings, troubles, and joys with others nurtures good mental health.

- *Give to others.* In giving of your time, talents, and money to others, you turn your thoughts away from yourself.

- *Show up every day.* Stress, disappointments, and grief can make us want to retreat, but as soon as you are able to return to participating in life, do so. Count your blessings. This is God's will for your life: "We know that in all things God works for the good of those who love him, who have been called according to his purpose . . . If God is for us, who can be against us?" (Romans 8:28, 31).

*Tips for Controlling Your Anger:*

- Acknowledge that it's time to ask for help, because we can only change something if we first acknowledge that it is a problem.

- Find a counselor you trust and to whom you will be accountable.

- Share with your husband that you need his help with the children, the house, and you personally. If you are not married, find someone to help you with the day-to-day stress that is pushing you to the breaking point.

- Examine your daily schedule to locate your most likely "trouble times." Children will misbehave if they are over-tired, not fed on time, or haven't had your attention for a while. It is not fair to lose your temper with your fussing child when his fussing is due to basic needs not being met. Create a routine that is good for your child's needs, and plan some downtime every day.

❋ Reevaluate your expectations of your child. Some children can sit in a doctor's office quietly, while others are climbing the walls in five minutes. Having unrealistic expectations of your child causes everyone to become angry. Recognize the difference between childishness (accidentally spilling milk) and defiance (throwing the cup).

❋ Don't overdo. You can't do every good thing *and* raise your children. Learn to say "No" to some things so that your life doesn't become full of chaos and strife.

❋ Take care of yourself. That's what this chapter is all about! If we stay up late every night, there is no way we'll have the patience or kindness to handle busy toddlers. It's trite but true: eating well, exercising, and getting enough sleep increase a woman's ability to handle daily stress. Moms also need regularly scheduled time alone. We only have our children for a season. Be the best mom you can be in this season of your life.

*Tips for Reducing Stress and Anxiety:*

❋ *Practice deep breathing.* At least once a day, sit quietly and do nothing but breathe in and out slowly and deeply. Take a deep beath in for a count of five and slowly exhale for a count of five. Focus on the sound and feel of your breathing. You want to breathe deeply for at least five minutes, slowing your breathing down to six breaths a minute.

❋ *Laugh and have fun!* Did you know that laughter is one of the quickest ways to release tension and help you relax? Find something to laugh about every day.

❋ *Focus on the positive.* Be a mom who rises above her circumstances. It's so easy to complain about the rain, fussy children, and endless meals to prepare. We are the thermostats for our homes, and our attitudes affect everyone.

- ✸ *Clean up the clutter.* Your surroundings influence your mental state more than you realize. A home that is cluttered with too much "stuff" only aggravates feelings of stress.

- ✸ *Let the sunshine in.* Increase the amount of light in your home. Invest in warm lights, open the shades during the day. Paint with light, nurturing colors. Bright, open space is conducive to clear, positive thinking.

- ✸ *Get enough sleep and rest.* When we sleep, our bodies heal and recharge. Eliminate caffeine after 4:00 p.m. Go to sleep and wake up at the same time every day, and stay away from upsetting stimuli just before bedtime.

- ✸ *Express your feelings.* Emotions need regular venting. Stuck, unexpressed emotions are the building blocks of pain and illness.

- ✸ *Be a lover!* Loving others and being in love are wonderful stress reducers. Pour on the love to your husband, friends, family, neighbors, etc. Ask God to open your eyes to someone He wants you to reach out and love. When you give to another, you will receive back even more.

*Tips on Overcoming Depression:*

- ✸ *Develop a strategy.* You must do something to help yourself crawl out of the darkness. Make a list of what you can do, and what others can do, for you to get better. Then take just that first step . . . and then the next.

- ✸ *Visit your doctor.* See if your depression has a medical explanation. Many times an undetected illness or chemical imbalance is the reason we feel depressed.

- ✸ *See a counselor.* Surround yourself with supportive people: "Medication plus some form of talk therapy has proven to be a highly effective combination in treating depression," says Dr. Isadore Rosenfeld.

- *Stop negative thinking.* Negative thoughts fuel depression. Counter them by thinking positive thoughts (Philippians 4:8–9), and give over the depression-causing problems to the Lord.

- *Speak words of life.* Just speaking negative words can pull us down into depression. When we complain, we are showing that we don't trust God enough to take care of our family or us.

- *Do go through the motions.* Try to function as best as you can. Find someone to hold you accountable. If you can, get out of bed, get up, get dressed, and do your work! Doing this will not take the pain completely away, but it will tell your depression that there is hope that one day soon you will not think these thoughts anymore.

- *Embrace the pain.* One of the verses that helped me when I was going through depression was Psalm 119:71: "It was good for me to be afflicted so that I might learn your decrees." This verse helped me seek and accept what good there was in the pain and be thankful in everything (1 Thessalonians 5:18).

- *Rest in God.* No thing and no one can heal your depression and all that is causing it; only God can do this: "I will give you the treasures of darkness, riches stored in secret places, so that you may know that I am the LORD, the God of Israel, who summons you by name" (Isaiah 45:3).

Remember, it is largely how we interpret the events and demands around us that determine how stressful they become for us. When you get smart about organizing the stress in your life, the immediate benefit will be a healthier, happier, more maintenance-free you.

# Set a Good Example

One of the most important lessons we need to teach our children is how to handle stress, disappointment, and crisis. When we set a good example for our children, they grow into adults who are mentally stable and healthy. If one of your children is overly emotional, teach her good coping skills. Then, when a crisis happens in your life, show her how you also must use these skills. One example of the way I handle stress or a crisis is the volume level of my voice. I naturally speak very loud, but I try to talk softly and precisely when I am upset, to calm down the situation.

Don't be afraid to let someone know when you are having a hard time in your life. We all need help now and then. Asking your children for help is another way to set a good example, and children naturally love to know ways to be helpful.

# Stress Busters!

Life is stressful—but we can use stress and its negative effects as a wake-up call. God does not want us to worry. He says to be "anxious for nothing" and that means *nothing*. Practice some of the "Stress Busters" listed below. They really do work. The fundamental stress busters to practice always are: eat a healthy diet, exercise regularly, get enough sleep, keep praying, and give all your concerns over to the Lord. Beyond these basics, try one of these this week.

- ☀ Buy yourself some flowers! Researchers have found that women who kept brightly colored flowers in their workspaces were less stressed than women who kept simple green plants without flowers.

&#9880; Vent your thoughts on paper. This is a fabulous way to let out your frustration without hurting anyone with your words. Researchers are discovering that the practice of journaling can reduce pain, help with weight loss, and even ease serious stress. "Writing may produce changes in immune or hormonal responses to stress, and improve relationships and our capacity to cope with stress," says Joshua M. Smyth, a psychologist at Syracuse University.

&#9880; Plan a short outing or a weekend trip; having something to look forward to is a great stress buster.

&#9880; Rent a "chick flick," curl up under a blanket with popcorn, and enjoy the time out.

&#9880; On a sunny day, take a book and a blanket outside and read. The combination of sunshine and vitamin D helps elevate our mood.

&#9880; Do something you have always wanted to do but never got around to, or were afraid to try.

 *Bringing It Home*

The more we understand how our thinking affects our role as a mom, the better mother we can become for our family. When we are positive, the whole family is more positive. Your attitude will either make you or break you, it's that important. When you rid your mind of mental "clutter," other aspects of life will fall into place.

Here are this chapter's main points:

&#9880; What you think and what you expose your mind to greatly affects who you are and who your children will become.

❀ Good mental health is not allowing yourself to be controlled by anxiety, anger, depression, unforgiveness, worry, or fear.

❀ Focus on what is good in your life, so that you can be a godly example for your children.

I pray that you have found other ways to make your mind healthier and stronger. There are so many benefits for mothers who are mentally organized and focused. When we are healthy mentally, our actions and words will be those that foster life. We will be better able to nurture our children, and they will grow up strong and ready to face life. Most of all, our Christian witness will be light in a dark world. We will be able to serve the Lord and others.

## True Love Heals

*Love is patient*
*Love is kind*
*Love does not envy*
*Love does not boast*
*Love is not proud*
*Love is not rude*
*Love is not self-seeking*
*Love is not easily angered*
*Love keeps no record of wrong*
*Love rejoices with the truth*
*Love always protects*
*Love always trusts*
*Love always hopes*
*Love always perseveres*
    *—from 1 Corinthians 13:4–7*

Moms, if we remember these words, and live by them, our families will be healthier and stronger, and our world will be a better place.

---

*Whatever is true, whatever is honorable, whatever is right, whatever is pure, whatever is lovely, whatever is of good repute, if there is any excellence and if anything worthy of praise, dwell on these things.*

—Philippians 4:8, NASB

---

 ## Plan of Action

Moms, if you are like me, your first plan of action is to go, go, go! I usually feel that everything important should have been done yesterday, and before I know it I am running in circles and only adding more stress to my life. I realized one day that, when Jesus was in His ministry, He didn't rush around trying to do everything. He didn't feed *all* the hungry, heal *all* the sick, or raise *all* the dead. He walked by people who were suffering every day. There was always more He could have done. Why didn't He do everything? When He came to the end of His life's work just before His crucifixion, Jesus said, "I have brought you glory on earth by completing the work you gave me to do" (John 17:4). Even though there was more to do, Jesus did just what God wanted Him to do.

Think about how exhausted you are at the end of some days. Did you try to exceed your limits? Jesus knew what His Father's will was, and He kept the stress level balanced. God knows just how much we can handle. He never overloads us, but neither does He promise us strength for tasks that we take on without His direction. Abide in Him, because apart from Him we can do nothing.

I also remember reading in the Gospels how stressed, anxious, depressed, and afraid the disciples were after Jesus died. They stayed together in the upper room, behind doors that were bolted shut because of their fear and stress over the past few days. But Jesus appeared through the walls and said, "Peace be with you" (John 20:19). This Jesus, who endured the same hurts, abuse, and rejection you may have experienced, had the power to conquer death and be with His disciples. No door or person could keep Him away! This same Jesus wants to enter the dark and fearful areas of your life, heal you, and lead you on a great mission, too.

These fearful, ignorant, uneducated men were completely transformed into vibrant, courageous men of God who left that locked room and went out into a lost world, changing history and lives forever. Let Him do the same for and through you.

For our tenth step to becoming a more organized mom, we have focused on the need to "Renew Your Mind." Where do you want to grow in your mental health? How do you want to get there, with God's help? Now look back at your response to Question #7 in the "Personal Inventory" section. Do you still agree with what you wrote and the order of importance you gave your three ideas? If you do, then complete the sentence below by writing in your #1 choice. Or, create a new #1 choice based on all that you've learned in this chapter.

With God's help I want to _____.

I think I will have to change _____ in order to make this happen. I'm ready to step out in faith with God and make this change so that my mind can be renewed in God.

# Step 11
## Revive Your Spirit

**"Like newborn babies, crave pure spiritual milk,**
**so that by it you may grow up in your salvation,**
**now that you have tasted that the Lord is good."**
**—1 Peter 2:2–3**

This chapter is the culmination of our study on becoming a stronger, healthier, more organized mom. As you looked at your physical and mental health in the last two chapters, I hope you realized how important these aspects of life are in relation to your role as a mom. When your body and mind become stronger and more organized, you can better organize your everyday life, which greatly benefits your children.

As you work toward becoming a healthier mom, I want to share with you that the most important aspect of your general health is *spiritual health:* nothing is more important than being strong spiritually. As the verse that introduces this chapter states, God wants us to be hungry and eager for His truth and His ways, just as a newborn child craves his mother's milk.

Most of us eat enough each day, so we aren't starving physically. And mentally and emotionally most of us are getting by okay. But I believe that almost every person on earth is starving spiritually. We feel hunger pains when our bodies need food, and we get "mental pains" when we begin to feel sad and down. But when God is trying to get our attention to slow down and turn to Him for nourishment, we sinful human beings tend to ignore the signals and continue on our merry, depleted way. While the food we feed our bodies lasts only a few hours, feeding our spirits lasts for eternity.

We are all spiritual beings. We are all created in the image of God for fellowship with Him and for His glory. When we walk with Him daily, as Adam and Eve did in the Garden of Eden, we experience a sense of peace and joy that are beyond comprehension. When we don't walk in His ways but launch out on our own, as Adam and Eve did when they were expelled from the Garden, we experience problems in every aspect of life.

The fact that there will be storms in life should not surprise us. Jesus knew this when He said, "In this world you will have trouble. But take heart! I have overcome the world" (John 16:33). God will give us the grace and ability to get through the storms of life, which threaten to destroy our spiritual health. He can make "all things to work together for good to those who love God, to those who are called according to His purpose" (Romans 8:28 NASB). He promises to never leave you or forsake you (Hebrews 13:5). We just need to seek Him and we will find Him (Jeremiah 29:13). When we admit that we cannot heal ourselves, and we fall to our knees and ask God to take over, we are on the road to reviving our spirits and our spiritual health. Rick Warren, author of the best-selling book *The Purpose-Driven Life,* observed in an interview (found online at http://www.billygraham.org/DMag_Article .asp?ArticleID=492) that life on earth is not so much about *what we do* as *who we are:*

> *In a nutshell, life is preparation for eternity. . . . Am I going to live for possessions? Popularity? Am I going to be driven by pressures? Guilt? Bitterness? Materialism? Or am I going to be driven by God's purposes? When I get up in the morning, I sit on the side of my bed and say, "God, if I don't get anything done today, I want to know You more and love You better." At*

*the end of the day, if I've done that, the day was a success. On the other hand, if I get to the end of the day and I haven't gotten to know God better and love Him more, I just missed the first purpose of life, and I've wasted the day. God didn't put me on earth just to fulfill a to-do list. He's more interested in who I am than what I do. That's why we're called human beings, not human doings.*

In the Old Testament the prophet Elijah came to a point in his life when he was completely empty—physically, emotionally, and spiritually. But God knew what Elijah's needs were, just as He knows your needs and mine. He sent an angel to Elijah to help him: "Get up and eat," said the angel, "for the journey is too much for you" (1 Kings 19:7). Moms, the journey of raising godly children is too great for you. Rest in the arms of the Shepherd, learn from Him, and grow in His strength. Remember that all of us at one time or another experience problems that won't go away. When they come, we are tempted to pray, "Lord, get me out of this mess." But the Lord permits many of the difficult situations we experience in our lives in order to grow our character into the image of His Son. So the Lord may be saying to you, "Let Me into this mess. Permit Me to change you rather than your circumstances." When you realize that circumstances in your life here on earth occur so that a miracle can happen, then you are developing spiritual strength. Let's look at what you need to grow strong spiritually.

*Create a special, yours-only, quiet place.* I became a Christian when I was twenty-three years old. I had gone to church before then, because my parents were very faithful in taking all seven children to Sunday school and church. But as an adult I came to see that becoming a Christian isn't so much about church attendance as it is about humbling ourselves before Almighty God, asking for forgiveness, and living our earthly lives loving and growing in the knowledge of our Savior.

After I made the choice to follow Jesus, I began to attend Bible studies and have a "quiet time" each day. I was taught that, in order to grow as a Christian, we all need time to get to know

Christ; the best way to do this is to study His Word, pray, fellowship with other believers, and spend time alone with Him. At that time I was single and had my devotional time at night in bed.

After I got married, I couldn't have my quiet time in bed anymore because the light bothered my husband and he couldn't sleep. So I began having my quiet time in our tiny bathroom—there was already a built-in seat! I guess I could have gone downstairs to our den, but I liked being close by to my husband, and later to our sleeping children.

We had been married about sixteen years when we moved to Colorado. There, we were able to buy a wonderful home in the foothills that had a large master bathroom. This bathroom had a fireplace and a whirlpool bathtub with a picture window that overlooked the mountains and valley! I placed a chair in the corner for my quiet-time place. There was room on both sides of my chair for books, Bibles, pens, notebooks, journals, etc. It was my heaven on earth.

I was teaching a neighborhood Bible study at the time, and mentioned the importance of having a place of your own for prayer and reading the Bible. One day, two of the ladies said it was time for them to see what I was talking about, so I brought them to my home. There, in my large bathroom was my little folding card table chair. "Lane, you need a chair that is comfortable and looks better!" they exclaimed. One of them owned an antique store, so we went looking for a chair. I found one in her dusty storage shed that was in such bad shape that it was half price. I bought it and had it recovered, and I still have it today.

The reason I go into such detail about my quiet-time space is that after I made it comfortable and inviting, I began to spend more time there every day and could feel the presence of the Lord more than ever. I would go into the bathroom to put away folded towels or clothes and would have a desire to sit in the chair to say a quick prayer. Or at times during the day I would go there to read God's Word a little bit. Nothing dramatic, but I knew God was meeting me there. Jesus said, "I am the vine; you are the branches" (John 15:5); if you want to increase your spiritual strength and grow deeper roots as one of the branches, then create your own special quiet place. It will change your life!

*Build intimacy with God through prayer.* God created us for intimacy and companionship with others. That's why we feel so empty inside when we are disconnected from other people. God also created us for intimacy and companionship with Him. It's as if we all have a great big empty hole deep within our souls that can only be filled by God Himself.

Jesus understood loneliness. He surely must have felt it when His disciples deserted Him before He was crucified. But in their absence God's presence sustained Him: "Yet I am not alone, for my Father is with me" (John 16:32). That intimacy with the Lord is the key to feeling a sense of wholeness, and it's available to all who put their trust in Him.

To begin instilling the habit of prayer, go to your special quiet-time place every day. Even if you only have sixty seconds, go there and pray. Then begin to remind yourself to pray when you wake up each morning, as you go through the day, and before you go to sleep at night. Ladies, praying while you're driving in the car is good, but you really need quiet time alone that is totally focused on God. He tells us to "be still, and know that I am God" (Psalm 46:10).

I know that when you first consider making time to pray, amidst all the diaper changing, dinner cooking, working, and chauffeuring, this idea may seem impossible. But being "still" in prayer means more than idly waiting for God to act; it means trusting that the Lord is in control, no matter what.

Below are a few Scripture citations from God's Word that affirm the life-transforming power you will receive when you spend time in prayer each day (adapted from Christian Broadcasting Network [CBN], *Seven Days Ablaze*, 2003):

* Prayer keeps a direct, intimate line of communication open between you and God: "The LORD is near to all who call on him, to all who call on him in truth" (Psalm 145:18).

- Prayer helps us gain inner peace and lifts feelings of depression and confusion: "Do not be anxious about anything, but in everything, by prayer and petition, with thanksgiving, present your requests to God. And the peace of God, which transcends all understanding, will guard your hearts and your minds in Christ Jesus" (Philippians 4:6–7).

- Prayer allows us to receive guidance from God to lead us in every aspect of life: "Call to me, and I will answer you and tell you great and unsearchable things you do not know" (Jeremiah 33:3).

- Prayer enables us to hear God speaking in our hearts through the Holy Spirit: "But the Counselor, the Holy Spirit, whom the Father will send in my name will teach you all things, and will remind you of everything I have said to you" (John 14:26).

- Prayer strengthens our faith in God and reassures us of His love: "The prayer of a righteous man is powerful and effective" (James 5:16).

- Prayer empowers us to resist Satan's temptations and win battles of spiritual warfare: "Be strong in the Lord and in his mighty power. Put on the full armor of God so that you can take your stand against the devil's schemes" (Ephesians 6:10–11).

- Prayer gives us confidence and assurance that God will answer our prayers: "If you remain in me and my words remain in you, ask whatever you wish, and it will be given you" (John 15:7).

Moms, we are told to "pray continually" (1 Thessalonians 5:17). When we pray, we build up our spiritual health and strength.

*Study God's Word.* The psalmist said of God's Word, "Your word is a lamp to my feet and a light for my path" (Psalm 119:105). Moms, we will never be able to accomplish the good things we want for our families *unless* we receive direction from the Lord, which is found in His Word. Paul wrote about this very thing: "Likewise, teach the older women to be reverent in the way they live, not to be slanderers or addicted to much wine, but to teach what is good. Then they can train the younger women to love their husbands and children, to be self-controlled and pure, to be busy at home, to be kind, and to be subject to their husbands, so that no one will malign the word of God" (Titus 2:3–5).

Moms, the Bible is alive! "The word of God is living and active. Sharper than any double-edged sword, it penetrates even to dividing soul and spirit, joints and marrow; it judges the thoughts and attitudes of the heart" (Hebrews 4:12). When we read the Bible, its truths penetrate deep into our souls, revealing what is right and what our real thoughts and intentions are.

The most valuable possession you will ever own on this earth is your Bible. It is God's gift to us to help us understand Him, ourselves, and our world. Find your Bible! If you don't own one, go to a Christian bookstore and ask a salesperson to help you choose the translation that is best for you. Or, go to your church and ask for one. Read your Bible every day. Just as having a specific place for quiet time is vital for growing and maintaining spiritual strength, so also reading God's Word. If you don't have a specific time set aside for structured Bible study, then read two Psalms and a chapter in Proverbs every day (since there are thirty-one chapters in Proverbs, you can read the chapter that coincides with the day of the month).

*Express gratitude each day.* The great sixteenth-century theologian Martin Luther once experienced a long period of worry and despondency. One day his wife put on black mourning clothes, and the following conversation took place:

*"Who died?" asked Luther.*

*"God," said his wife.*

*"God!" said Luther, horrified. "How can you say such a thing?"*

*She replied, "I'm only saying what you are living."*

Luther realized that indeed he was living as if God were no longer alive and watching over them in love. When this happened, he quickly changed his outlook from gloom to gratitude. The Bible says that we are to "be joyful always; pray continually; give thanks in all circumstances, for this is God's will for you in Christ Jesus" (1 Thessalonians 5:16–18).

Don't we all go through times when we live as if God were dead? We start to worry and become despondent as the problems of life pile up. Dear mom, when you are tempted to despair and stop trusting in the goodness of God, remember that our Savior, Jesus Christ, knows firsthand about grief, temptation, and pain that ends in death. Read through the Psalms. Some of the psalmists faced bleak times, but even in spite of these they all gave thanks to God in the midst of their trials. For example, David wrote, "You turned my wailing into dancing; you removed my sackcloth and clothed me with joy, that my heart may sing to you and not be silent. O LORD my God, I will give you thanks forever" (Psalm 30:11–12).

Meeting every situation with thanksgiving isn't a denial of reality. What it does is help us see those situations from God's perspective. Trials are opportunities to discover God's power, mercy, and love; they help us develop our character so that it becomes more Christ-like. Every time you choose to trust God in the midst of a difficult situation, you are declaring, "God is alive and He is able to take care of me!"

God's Word is very clear about how we are to respond to difficulties and fears. We are to focus on what is good, be grateful, and count our blessings. Why? Because God knows that trusting in His goodness and power is the key to turning tragedy into triumph. Dr. Charles Stanley offers four reasons why praise is the best response to hardship:

1. Giving thanks to God keeps us continually aware of His presence.

2. Giving thanks motivates us to seek God's will and plan for our lives.

3. Giving thanks teaches us to become more submissive to God's will.

4. Giving thanks even in the midst of suffering teaches us to trust God.

Each of us chooses each day the way we will respond to life's bumps and bruises. We can choose to be complaining, upset, or worried. Or we can choose to believe that God is good and trustworthy, despite all outward appearances, "for this is God's will for you in Christ Jesus" (1 Thessalonians 5:18). Moms, when we have toilets to clean, we can be thankful we have a family that gets them dirty. When we have clothes to wash, we can be thankful we have clothes to wear and water in which to clean them. When we have to clean up after a party, we can be thankful we have friends to be with and a home for them to visit. When we have a huge heating bill to pay, we can be thankful we have heat to keep us warm. When we are stuck in traffic, we can be thankful we have a car. When our baby has an ear infection, *again,* we can be thankful we have reliable doctors and available medicine to relieve her pain. When our husband has to travel for work, we can be thankful he has a job. And when our teenager is complaining about everything, we can be thankful we have a child.

You may be in a situation that is so painful it seems impossible to find anything at all to thank God for. What can you do? You can tell God that you can't even pray, and then ask Him to pray for you through His Holy Spirit. The moment you became a Christian, God sent His Holy Spirit to dwell within you and to empower you. He will give you the strength to glorify God even in your darkest hour. You can say, "Thank you. I know You love me and are in control of my life." and walk through the fire. You will become the person and the mom God has called you to be. Your life will have an impact on your family, friends, coworkers, and the world, becoming a light for them to follow.

*Recognize spiritual warfare.* One of the most important lessons we need to learn if we are to stay spiritually strong and healthy is that we have an enemy. In 1 Peter 5:8 we are warned to "be self-controlled and alert. Your enemy the devil prowls around like a roaring lion looking for someone to devour." This enemy wants you to be depressed and full of guilt. It doesn't even matter what causes you to feel so down, he just wants to do everything he can to take your eyes off God. But Scripture promises that "there is now no condemnation for those who are in Christ Jesus" (Romans 8:1). When you and I are in Christ, we are not condemned anymore! We may stumble again and again, but when we ask for forgiveness, we are not condemned. That's freedom!

You see, the Enemy attacks us when and where we are defenseless. While he is not omniscient, he knows just enough to work against us—like when we're in the middle of P.M.S. or we have an important meeting that can't be missed. He will do anything in his power to take our minds off the Lord, even during prayer. He exploits times of loneliness, tiredness, and other vulnerabilities.

The Enemy works to create doubt in our minds. He wants us to question the truth of God's Word and feel unsure about our salvation. Once disbelief and doubt set in, as it did for Adam and Eve (Genesis 3:1–6), our minds begin twisting the meaning of Scripture to justify our conduct.

While we are susceptible to the schemes of the devil, we are not helpless (2 Timothy 1:7). Our heavenly Father protects us, our Savior intercedes for us, and the Holy Spirit guides us to the truth. Our part is to make sure we adhere to God's Word, pray, make good choices, and put on God's armor for battle.

Battle? Armor? Yes, there is a spiritual war going on around us that is more dangerous than physical warfare, though we often ignore or do not fully understand it. As I mentioned above, we have a powerful enemy working against us. Paul called him "the god of this age" (2 Corinthians 4:4) because he is the source of evil and wickedness in our world. To overcome his attacks we must recognize that he is a real adversary, and we need to protect ourselves against him with spiritual armor:

> *Finally, be strong in the Lord and in his mighty power. Put on the full armor of God so that you can take your stand against the devil's schemes. For our struggle is not against flesh and blood, but against the rulers, against the authorities, against*

> *the powers of this dark world and against the spiritual forces of evil in the heavenly realms. Therefore, put on the full armor of God, so that when the day of evil comes, you may be able to stand your ground, and after you have done everything, to stand. Stand firm then, with the belt of truth buckled around your waist, with the breastplate of righteousness in place, and with your feet fitted with the readiness that comes from the gospel of peace. In addition to all this, take up the shield of faith, with which you can extinguish all the flaming arrows of the evil one. Take the helmet of salvation and the sword of the Spirit, which is the word of God. And pray in the Spirit on all occasions with all kinds of prayers and requests. With this in mind, be alert and always keep on praying for all the saints. (Ephesians 6:10–18)*

Moms, we have to be armed in order to protect both ourselves and our families.

I know that for some of you the thought of spiritual warfare is somewhat scary. But I want you to know the truth about what you are up against, so you will begin to intercede for yourself and your family. God does not want us to live in fear, for "God did not give us a spirit of timidity, but a spirit of power, of love and of self-discipline" (2 Timothy 1:7). God richly blesses those who live by faith and do not give in to the scarecrows of doubt and fear: "For though we live in the world, we do not wage war as the world does. The weapons we fight with are not the weapons of the world. On the contrary, they have divine power to demolish strongholds. We demolish arguments and every pretension that sets itself up against the knowledge of God, and we take captive every thought to make it obedient to Christ" (2 Corinthians 10:3–5).

The Enemy's goal is to keep the true knowledge of God from us. If you are a believer in Christ, the Enemy knows he has already lost you for eternity, so he tries to ruin this life on earth while he can. He will play to our individual sins and temptations and create a "stronghold" in your life. A stronghold is a pattern that becomes so entrenched in your heart that you perform it habitually, not even recognizing that you are exhibiting un-Christ-like behavior, or that you can choose to resist. You *do* have a choice!

When we understand the way a stronghold can pull us down, we can turn to God and live in victory. We can become the moms our children need, discerning and teaching them about the difference between truth and lies. The following lists are from *The Building Up and the Tearing Down of Strongholds,* by Anabel Gillham.

*Truths: I know that . . .*

- ☀ Christ dwells in me.
- ☀ I am loved/accepted/a new creation.
- ☀ I have given my problem to the Lord.
- ☀ Christ, dwelling within me, can meet whatever lies ahead victoriously.
- ☀ "I can do all things through Christ who strengthens me . . ."
- ☀ My only hope is to allow Him to meet each event.
- ☀ This time on earth is a very short time.
- ☀ I am IN Christ—resting, secure, loved, accepted, empowered!

*Lies: Satan says that . . .*

- ☀ I cannot go on.
- ☀ I am going to be destroyed.
- ☀ I am alone.
- ☀ I am a loser.
- ☀ I'll never be able to do anything.
- ☀ There is no hope for me.

In the 1700s, William Cowper noted that "Satan trembles when he sees the weakest saint upon his knees."

*Implement the truth.* I read a story about a man in New York City who died at the age of sixty-three without ever having had a job. He spent his entire adult life in college, acquiring many degrees. Why did this man spend his entire life this way? When he was a child, a wealthy relative died and named him the primary beneficiary in his will. It stated that he was to be given enough money to support him every year as long as he stayed in school. And it was to be discontinued when he completed his education.

The man met the terms of the will but, by staying in school indefinitely, he turned a technicality into a steady income for life—something his benefactor never intended to happen. Unfortunately, he spent thousands of hours listening to professors and reading books but never "doing" anything. He acquired more and more knowledge, but he *didn't put it into practice.*

This last section in becoming a more organized mom through becoming spiritually strong is very important. You and I can read books and listen to sermons and speakers, yet remain stagnant and unchanged. If we fail to put to work what we have learned, we are as guilty as the man with all the "head" knowledge. His education was of no practical benefit to anyone. What we need to do is *apply* the truth that we hear: "Do not merely listen to the word, and so deceive yourselves. Do what it says" (James 1:22). When we implement the truth, we grow into stronger women of God.

Where does organization come in? Well, if you implement some of the suggestions and ideas about how to become more organized, you will experience less stress and more time to grow into the woman God created you to be. You will be able to see more clearly and focus on what is really important. Then you can be a "doer of the Word." Then, like Paul, you can say, "I press on toward the goal to win the prize for which God has called me" (Philippians 3:14). This is our goal, moms: to live our lives in a way that glorifies our Lord.

*What we do, more than anything we say,*
*reveals what we truly value the most.*

—David McCasland

# Personal Inventory

Your spiritual health is a very personal, individual matter. But taking the time to review your personal inventory can greatly increase your awareness of where you are in your walk with the Lord. As I mentioned earlier, taking an "Inventory" helps us acknowledge where we are and where we want to go. Perhaps before you fill out the inventory, you might want to go to your quiet place so you will have time to concentrate and reflect.

1. Describe your ideal quiet-time place. What do you need to do to create such a place for yourself?

   _____

   _____

2. How would you describe your prayer life right now?

   _____

   _____

3. What do you enjoy about studying the Bible? What is challenging for you about Bible study?

   _____

   _____

4. Below is a list of feelings that people typically use to measure their spiritual health. Place a check mark beside all that apply to you.

   ❑ Feel hunger to know God and His truth

   ❑ Experience an increasing awareness of my sin

   ❑ Feel sincere repentance and the desire to become more like Christ

- ❑ View trials, temptations, and failures as avenues that lead to growth
- ❑ Desire to be used by God in the lives of others
- ❑ Desire to obey God, regardless of the personal cost
- ❑ Experience increasing faith in God
- ❑ Feel hunger for private devotion, Bible study, fellowship, and prayer
- ❑ Desire to make decisions based on God's will and not on personal wants
- ❑ Feel vibrant love for God and awareness of His presence

5. Below are examples of sins that *can become* strongholds for Satan to weaken our devotion to God. Check any that you feel may be present in your life.

- ❑ Pride
- ❑ Complacency
- ❑ Envy
- ❑ Gossip
- ❑ Slander
- ❑ Hostility
- ❑ Indulgence
- ❑ Inferiority
- ❑ Self-condemnation
- ❑ Jealousy
- ❑ Covetousness
- ❑ Vanity
- ❑ Gluttony
- ❑ Perfectionism
- ❑ Rebelliousness
- ❑ Self-deprecation
- ❑ Self-pity
- ❑ Worry

6. Name three areas of your life where you want to begin seeking God first before everything else. Then number them in order of priority.

#____ _____

#____ _____

#____ _____

*God has conferred on motherhood a true nobility,*
*and she who gladly fills that role can shape man's destiny.*

—D. De Haan

 # Everybody Wins!

Moms, when we are walking in the Spirit of the Lord, everybody wins. When we are organized in our spiritual life, the fruits of the Spirit become evident and spill over onto our children, blessing and strengthening their lives. These fruits reveal what is within our heart. You can read about these fruits in Galatians 5:22–23: love, joy, peace, patience, kindness, goodness, faithfulness, gentleness, and self-control.

But, moms, when we are not organized in our spiritual health, everyone around us suffers with us. We lose hope, our sense of direction, our focus . . . and our children lose their purpose and direction.

I know that there are times when life is so difficult that it is hard even to pray to God, much less walk in His Spirit. Don't forget that you can count on the prayers of Jesus Himself! When

Jesus ascended after the resurrection, He went to the Father as our advocate (1 John 2:1). Picture Jesus praying for you right now, as well as the Holy Spirit, who "intercedes for us with groans that words cannot express" (Romans 8:26). Even when we are faced with an overwhelming problem, we can still win because we have Jesus and His power and might on our side.

## What I've Learned

As I mentioned in the last section, there may be times when the circumstances of your life feel so overwhelming that you can't even pray. This has happened to me many times, and what I've learned is that the Holy Spirit comforts us and prays for us during those times. I went through a time of such great loss, loneliness, and pain that I truly thought I would not survive. There was a two-year time period when *everything* in my life was changed or lost.

It began when my husband had to find a new job and we moved away from Colorado. This happened at the same time that I discovered a serious problem in our marriage. Our older daughter had just graduated from high school. Within three weeks we sold our dream home, she graduated, we moved across the country, and lived displaced—without roots—for three months, waiting for our new house to be ready. We were still living in a hotel when it came time for my older daughter to begin college. Saying good-bye to her felt like just one more loss. Then, as we were all driving to her college, she and our younger daughter were driving a car behind my husband and me, and it rolled over three times and crashed! I thought both daughters were gone. It was truly a miracle that we could get them out of the car, and they survived without any broken bones or even a stitch! A few months later my husband was gone. I was faced with starting life over in a new city, with no friends, and one daughter away at college; I felt as if everything I had ever known or been given had been taken from me.

I realized then that loneliness isn't only about the absence or loss of people; it's also about the loss of the familiar. My daughters and I lost a family we thought we were part of; we lost our church home, our friends, our neighbors, and our wonderful home. I went from being a homemaker who cooked a family dinner most nights of the week, to being a single mom who works outside the home. I needed to find a job, but I hadn't been in the workplace for over eighteen years. I became so despondent.

But it was then that I learned that when we are on our knees, God is there! I began to pray and read more. One book that was a tremendous comfort to me was Beth Moore's book *Praying God's Word.* Through reading God's Word and praying through Beth's book, I knew God was with me. He was there when I cried out to Him (Psalm 107:13), and He pulled me up out of the "miry clay." He says, "I will restore you to health and heal your wounds" (Jeremiah 30:17). And He has promised *always* to be with us. He wants us to fellowship with Him more than anything else, and we do that by spending time in prayer.

There is another verse that was and is so comforting to me. In Jeremiah 29:11–14 God explains that He is in control. He has a plan for us, even when everything around us is falling apart:

> *"For I know the plans I have for you," declares the* LORD, *"plans to prosper you and not to harm you, plans to give you hope and a future. Then you will call upon me and come and pray to me, and I will listen to you. You will seek me and find me when you seek me with all your heart. I will be found by you," declares the* LORD, *"and will bring you back from captivity."*

Moms, one thing I have learned is that God is God. God is powerful, and He loves us with an undying love. He will rescue us from whatever captivity we are in and restore us!

 *Try This . . .*

Maybe you aren't quite sure where to begin your quest for better spiritual health. Some of you are involved in a local church, and some of you have not found a church home where the gospel is taught. Keep asking the Lord to guide you as you check out churches in your area. As you take steps, God will lead you along the way. He wants you to seek Him: "I love those who love me, and those who seek me find me" (Proverbs 8:17).

Try some of these tips:

- ❀ If you feel you don't know how to pray, don't worry, neither did the disciples! They said, "Lord, teach us to pray just as John taught his disciples." Jesus taught His disciples a prayer we call the Lord's Prayer (Luke 11:1–4 and Matthew 6:9–13).

- ❀ Remember the word ACTS: each letter represents a word to help you pray.

  Adoration. We need to come to the Lord with praise for who He is.

  Confession. We then need to confess our sins before God.

  Thanksgiving. We need to give thanks to God for His blessings.

  upplication. Then we are ready to ask for what we need.

- ❀ Find a Bible study or Sunday school class to attend on a regular basis. Check with your church to see if they have a women's Bible study and, if not, ask where you might find one.

- ❀ Find a devotional you can use each day. One of my favorite devotionals is from *Walk Thru the Bible Ministries*. A devotional guide comes monthly with day-to-day readings, as well as explanations of what to read and ways to apply these Scriptures to your life; you read through the entire Bible in one year. The devotional I am now using, *Our Daily Bread,* has been blessing people since 1956.

✸ Have a place (a quiet-time place) where you can go to pray and study God's Word. Having your own "prayer closet" can change your life.

✸ Memorize Scripture, and memorize verses or short sections with your children. You will be amazed at how quickly they learn—and how they help *you* memorize! You can also write the verse you want to memorize on a 3 x 5 card so you can take it with you or place it in your kitchen window, on your desk at work, or in your car.

✸ Study Scripture, especially Psalms and Proverbs. Read the Bible in the morning and right before bedtime. The words of God will be in your subconscious as you sleep.

# Set a Good Example

Setting a good example for our children *is* hard. But if we are diligent about organizing our spiritual health, our children will definitely notice. As I have mentioned earlier, I had my quiet time at night. One evening my daughter Christi came walking into the bedroom with her Bible and said it was time for her Bible reading. She was only two years old! She had seen me read the Bible and wanted to do what her mother was doing! What's funny is that I never realized she noticed. This is why setting a good example in front of our children is so important. They see what we do, when we do it, and why we do it, and because we are their heroines, they want to copy everything we do. When we try to grow our own relationship with God, we are helping our children follow God in their lives. Don't let the times that you have not been a good example keep you from trying again. I have failed too. We can be good examples to our children in those times too, if we turn to God and trust Him.

 ## Stress Busters!

We all have times when our faith seems to fall into a "humdrum" mode. If this has happened to you, below are a few ideas that might help rekindle your love for God:

- Remember Who it is that you are praying to. When I focus on God and all He has done, I am brought back to the feeling of "first love" that I experienced when I first committed my life to Him (Revelation 2:4).

- Keep a Prayer Journal where you record your prayers. When God answers a prayer—sometimes with "Yes," sometimes with "No," and sometimes with "Not yet"—check it off and date it. You will be amazed when you look back at the end of the year and see all the prayers that God has answered. Another spin on this idea is to keep a Gratitude Journal that helps you stay focused on the positive side of life. List five things you are grateful for every day. Watch how this journal keeps you focused on what is good and positive in your life.

- Ask a girlfriend to pray for you and offer to pray for her. Rather than doubling your load, you'll actually lighten it!

- Listen to Christian music while you are driving in the car or making dinner. Music has such healing power! Singing and listening to Christian music can keep you on fire for the Lord.

- Give of your time and your resources. Have your family sponsor a missionary or a child in need.

- Read the Psalms every day. They are very uplifting and will build a spirit of praise into your day and also within you.

# *Bringing It Home*

How does your spiritual health relate to becoming a more organized mother? Well, how we act and what we think both shape, as well as reflect, our character. When our character is focused on all that is good (God's truth), good actions, habits, and behaviors are sure to follow. As we begin developing our spiritual health, we experience an outpouring of God's Spirit, His truth, and His ways to guide us. We become better focused and able to handle life's day-to-day responsibilities and difficulties. We become better examples to our children, as well as to those in our neighborhoods and communities. The good example you set is sure to influence others and the choices they make.

In this chapter we have looked at how . . .

- ❀ Becoming spiritually healthy needs to be our most important goal in life.

- ❀ God walks with us on this journey, promising never to leave us or forsake us (Hebrews 13:5).

- ❀ Making a conscious effort daily to incorporate Bible study, prayer, gratitude, and music keeps us spiritually strong.

*Praise is almost the only thing we do on earth
that we shall not cease to do in heaven.*

—Samuel Brengle

# *Plan of Action*

As with any goal, we have to have a plan of action. I hope some of the tips and thoughts in this chapter will help you make a plan of action to meet your own spiritual goals.

Author John Eldredge tells a story about a Scottish athlete in the nineteenth century who made an iron discus based on a description he had read in a book. What he didn't know was that the discus used in official competition was made of wood, with only an outer rim of iron. His was a solid metal discus that weighed three or four times as much as those being used by other discus throwers. The man marked out the record distance in a field near his home and trained day and night to match it. For years he labored, until he broke the record. Then he took his iron discus to England for his first competition. When he arrived at the games, he easily set a new record that was far beyond those of his competitors. He remained the uncontested champion for many years, all because he trained under a heavy burden and became better for it.

Moms, God wants to build us up each day into strong women of faith. When we are given a heavy burden to bear, we need to bear it in Jesus' strength and for His sake. Whatever the burden or suffering, God will use it to "perfect, establish, strengthen, and settle" us, as 1 Peter 5:10 (NKJV) says. Our burdens can make us better than we ever imagined—stronger, more patient, more courageous, more gentle, and more loving than we could otherwise be. My prayer is that you will become the best mom you can be. You can do it! "Be strong and courageous. Do not be terrified; do not be discouraged, for the LORD your God will be with you wherever you go" (Joshua 1:9).

For our eleventh step to becoming a more organized mom, we have focused on the need to "Revive Your Spirit." Where do you want to be in your spiritual growth? How do you want to get there, with God's help? Now look back at your response to Question #6 in the "Personal Inventory" section. Do you still agree with what you wrote and the order of importance you gave your three ideas? If you do, then complete the sentence below by writing in your #1 choice. If not, create a new #1 choice based on all you've learned and thought about in this chapter.

With God's help I want to _____.

I think I will have to change _____ in order to make this happen. I'm ready to step out in faith with God and make this change so God can revive my spirit with the knowledge of His grace and mercy.

*He who began a good work in you will carry it on to completion until the day of Christ Jesus.*

—Philippians 1:6

# Step 12
## Build a Strong Family

**"I press on toward the goal to win the prize
for which God has called me."
—Philippians 3:14**

As we have walked through the past eleven steps together, I have tried to share as much information, guidance, and hope as I possibly could. Our last step emphasizes the purpose behind these pages: building a strong family is the ultimate goal of every mother. To do that, moms need wisdom from the Lord and organizational helps in every aspect of our lives. If you set goals, plan, and organize your days, you will see great growth in your family. Your children, your husband, and *you* will become stronger.

Up to this point we have talked about how to manage our time, provide nutritious food, and nurture strong relationships with one another. We have discussed the different skills we need to teach our children, along with ways to discipline them effectively. Because life is often stressful and being a mom is difficult in itself, we have emphasized the need to recover a sense of our selves and to restore our bodies, minds, and spirits.

When we begin to work on applying all that we have learned, we are on the path to building a stronger family. God's desire is that our families flourish and become beacons of light for a lost world. In fact, God's first spoken command recorded in Scripture concerns the family: "Be fruitful and increase in number; fill the earth" (Genesis 1:28).

Mothers, stepmothers, grandmothers, married, single, or divorced, there isn't a more influential or powerful role anyone on earth can play than being a mother. Of all the adults who interact with our children, no one makes a greater impact or exerts greater influence over them than we do. When we realize how important we are to the growth and development of our families, we begin to understand the importance of organizing our time, talents, and jobs to better teach and influence our children.

## *Six Characteristics of Strong Families*

*1. They are committed to the family.*

*2. They spend time together.*

*3. They have good family communication.*

*4. They express appreciation for one another.*

*5. They have a commitment to spiritual development.*

*6. They are able to solve problems in a crisis.*

*—Professor Nick Stinnett,*
*Department of Human Development*
*and Family at the University of Nebraska*

 *Personal Inventory*

Moms, when we know where we are and where we want to be, we can make the changes needed to get there. This is the reason taking your "Personal Inventory" is such an important investment of your time. As you work through the questions below, answer them honestly so that you get a real sense of the current state of your family's strength. At the end of the chapter, when you make your "Plan of Action," you'll be able to see your next step and what you need to do to take it.

1. Name three things you are currently doing to strengthen your family's ties to one another.

    #1 _____

    #2 _____

    #3 _____

2. How often do you express daily appreciation to the members of your family? In what ways do you show them that you appreciate them?

    _____ x/day _____ x/week

    _____

    _____

3. What are three ways that your family could improve communication with one another? These might involve changing how each of you handles crisis situations; how you communicate expectations of behavior, demonstrate respect, etc.

    #1 _____

    #2 _____

    #3 _____

4. Do you try to spend time with each member of your family every day? What do you focus on, and how are you attentive to them?

   ❑ Yes

   ❑ No, because _____.

   _____

5. List three things you are not currently doing but could do in order to strengthen your ties with your husband and children. Number these in order of priority.

   #____ _____

   #____ _____

   #____ _____

---

*No child is poor who has had a godly mother.*

—Abraham Lincoln

---

 *Everybody Wins!*

Mom, I hope by now you see that everybody wins when we work hard to become better organized and diligently plan our family lives. If you first concentrate on becoming more organized in just one aspect of life, as you see the benefits of this change I believe you will be motivated to continue on the path outlined in this book. When we are organized, we can do the will of God more fully. When we are organized, our minds are sharper, our actions have purpose, and we accomplish our goals much more quickly.

Then, our family gains a more consistent and balanced lifestyle and home life. Our children, in turn, become more organized in their schoolwork, activities, and friendships.

All of us are bound by repetition as we go about our daily routines. Day after day we eat, work, clean up, take care of our children, and sleep. We can lose our enthusiasm for life when there is "nothing new under the sun" (Ecclesiastes 1:9). But it's important to understand that as we participate in these repetitive activities, character can be formed, faith can be deepened, hope can be heightened, and endurance can be strengthened—and this is true for both you and your children. Through the everydayness of life, God is saying to us that there is more to our earthly existence than the meaningless repetition of duties and concerns. We need to listen to Him!

Part of God's plan for us is that we yield to His guidance in ordinary events that occur over and over again. Repeatedly trusting the Lord throughout this hour, this day, this week, this month, this year, is by far the surest way to make life fresh and successful: "Therefore . . . stand firm. Let nothing move you. Always give yourselves fully to the work of the Lord, because you know that your labor in the Lord is not in vain" (1 Corinthians 15:58).

 *What I've Learned*

Over the past few years I have heard several versions of a 1920s story about a seasoned missionary couple who returned from India to their home in New York on furlough. Their ship arrived in New York harbor, where a crowd of people was awaiting an important dignitary coming in on that same ship. The missionaries had to wait to disembark until the dignitary made his way down the walkway. As he did, a band played and the crowd cheered and waved welcome signs. The missionaries watched the procession for a few moments, and then the husband turned to his wife and asked, "Why don't we get that kind of fanfare when we return home?" "Maybe we will," his wife replied. "We just haven't returned home yet."

What I have learned in my twenty-five years as a mother is that oftentimes what we *think* is important really isn't, in the long run. I tried so hard as a new mother to "get everything done" that I became stressed, tired, and irritable with my family. What purpose does this serve? Moms, our real home is in heaven! When I remember to focus on the eternal more than the temporal, my whole attitude changes. Yes, your family and home are important to you, but try not to forget why we have them in the first place. We are raising children for God, to live for His will and His glory. I've learned that when I remember where my true home is, I can tackle the obstacles here in this temporal home much more easily.

I have also learned that taking life slower, more laid-back, and calmer is so much more fun! Some of my best memories and joys are the times when the girls and I just kicked back and played together all day long. We loved to stay in our pajamas and play games and watch movies. We enjoyed walking together and taking trips. I loved reading to them at night or just lying on their beds listening to them talk. I tried to stop whatever chore I was doing when they needed me, because it helped keep my focus on them and not so much on tasks. When I kept my deadlines and chores up to date, I was able to be more available to my children, and that's the beauty—and purpose—of being a more organized mom.

If you are reading this chapter around the Christmas holidays, you'll appreciate the Christmas version of 1 Corinthians 13 below. But if not, there are plenty of other hectic times in the year you can imagine in the place of Christmas!

---

*If I decorate my house perfectly with plaid bows,*
*strings of twinkling lights, and shiny balls,*
*but do not show love to my family,*
*I am just another decorator.*

*If I slave away in the kitchen,*
*baking dozens of Christmas cookies,*
*preparing gourmet meals,*
*and arranging a beautifully adorned table at mealtime,*
*but do not show love to my family,*
*I am just another cook.*

*If I work at a soup kitchen,*
*sing carols in a nursing home,*
*and give all I have to charity,*
*but do not show love to my family,*
*it profits me nothing.*

*If I trim the spruce with shimmering angels and crystal snowflakes,*
*attend a myriad of holiday parties and sing in the choir's cantata,*
*but do not focus on Christ,*
*I have missed the point.*

*Love stops the cooking to hug the child or kiss the husband.*
*Love is kind, though harried or tired.*
*Love does not envy another's home that has*
*coordinated Christmas china and table linens.*
*Love doesn't yell at the kids or other family to get out of the way,*
*but is thankful that they are there to get in the way.*
*Love doesn't give only to those who are able to give in return,*
*but rejoices in giving to those who can't.*
*Love bears all things, believes all things, hopes all things,*
*endures all things.*
*Love never fails.*
*Video games will break, pearl necklaces will be lost,*
*and golf clubs will rust.*
*But giving the gift of love will endure forever.*

— *Author Unknown*

 *Try This . . .*

The best way to accomplish anything, moms, is to step out and try! (It's so much easier to turn the steering wheel when the car is moving!) Try some of these tips to get you moving toward building a stronger family.

- *Baby your baby.* They are little for such a short time! Look for ways to play and be with your baby, toddler, or young child. Give him or her hugs, kisses, and gentle caresses, and remember to say "I love you," throughout the day.

- *Structure your children's day.* Children have more security when they have a routine. Schedule times for eating, chores, fun, outings, quiet time, reading, and sleep.

- *Be flexible with your teenagers.* Adolescent years aren't anything like the early childhood years. In order for families to stay close and enjoy a fairly consistent level of harmony and unity through this time, you must be willing to be flexible. Parents who are secure and mature enough to negotiate, provide space, listen more than lecture, empower, and maintain an affirming attitude and a good sense of humor can look forward to some of the most exciting years.

- *Teach spiritual principles and virtues.* Teach—by word and example—virtues such as self-discipline, perseverance, responsibility, and honesty. These and many other moral attributes affect our lives and families in positive ways that last a lifetime.

- *Simplify your life.* Less really is more, ladies. Focus on the Lord and your family more, and think of things less.

- *Nurture your self and your relationships.* If you need to make peace with your husband, friend, or family member, do it now. Don't wait another day. When you are at peace

252

with your self and your loved ones, your family enjoys peace too.

☀ *Have a family devotional time.* When my girls were toddlers, I read to them before bedtime each night, and then we would pray together as a family. When they became older, I kept two books by the dinner table that we would take turns reading. The beauty of these books was that the message only took one minute to read: we were having "family devotions" that weren't long enough for anyone to protest!

 # *Set a Good Example*

Moms, I've been reminding you all along that your example is a powerful teacher to your children. Most often, it is not your words but your actions that speak loudest and longest. Children seem to have a sixth sense that tells them whether their family is strong or not. When you set a good example with your own habits and relationships, the benefits spill over into your family, helping your children grow into the strong adults we pray they will be.

I'm sure you want all of your children's relationships to be solid and successful, from great friendships to a great marriage. An example you can set for your children is to expose them to your circle of friends. Have your friends over for dinner, bridge, or movie night, so that your children can see how you treat your friends. They will see you make the house look inviting, prepare special treats to eat, welcome your friends warmly, and make sure they have a good time while in your home. For you single moms, choose another Christian family in your church or community to spend time with as families, especially if you have sons, so they can see and experience what a godly husband and father is like.

Another example you can model for your children is to live life with a positive attitude. When we are positive and confident, our children learn to handle adversity and crises much better. When we have a positive self-image, high self-esteem, and firmly trust in the goodness of God, we enjoy our parenting role more; and we can bend without breaking at times when things are out of control.

Let your children see you say "No" to the demands of others. Let them see you be assertive yet kind, and prioritize your goals. We set a wonderful example for our children when we are even-tempered (with some highs and lows!), are consistent with family rules and discipline, and affirm all that is good in them.

I know these things sound like a tall order, but the basis of setting a good example for your children is maintaining your trust in God, no matter what happens. Remember, moms, you will only have your children for a short time. If you live to be eighty, only about twenty of those years will be focused on child rearing. Enjoy these years! Your children will be out on their own before you know it.

© BIL KEANE, INC. KING FEATURES SYNDICATE

# Stress Busters!

Like it or not, we moms set the tone in our homes. You have probably noticed that when you are in control of your well-being and responsibilities, your children are much easier to keep under control. By the same token, when you are upset, your children act up more. Children are little thermometers, responding to the emotional temperature in the home. You may be thinking that, when you get stressed, it's impossible to keep it together. I know exactly what you mean! So here are some stress busters that I hope will be helpful as you strive to make your family stronger.

- Try walking away from a stressful situation, to give yourself time to calm down and analyze what is really going on. When you are ready to return to the situation, you'll be able to respond much more effectively, because you won't be reacting out of frustration or anger.

- Pick a day this week when you absolutely refuse to do any work around the house—not even cook dinner. Instead, use the time to play with your husband/a friend and your children. Board games, card games, walks, movies, manicures, and—my favorite—naps are all fair game! (My girls loved it when I would play Mario with them because I was so bad at it!)

- Having tried the suggestion above and seen how much better you feel, create a "playtime" once a week. Spend part of the day with your children and the other part with a girlfriend or by yourself.

- Declare one night a week "family night." This is a great time for pizza and a movie, or hamburgers and board games, etc.

# Bringing It Home

Moms, when you apply organizational principles to your life, you naturally build a stronger family. Think back to those times when you began a new job. You needed to understand your role within the company. You needed to understand how your job related to the goals of the company. You probably thought through the steps you needed to take in order to reach those goals. If you worked hard, diligently, consistently, and with a positive outlook, you probably became successful in doing that job. Well, our job as mothers is no different. We need to understand our job description, as well as the role each family member plays in achieving the overall goals. We need to plan and organize our family life to meet those goals. We need to take breaks, holidays, and vacations. We need to set priorities, have (family) conferences, and establish a written "Daily Work Planner" (calendar or "To Do" list) with our families, just as we would do in any other job.

If your goal is to nurture, love, teach, train, and guide your children to become competent, well-adjusted, godly adults, you must have a plan. That awareness is the goal of this chapter as well as this book.

Let's recap the main points in this chapter:

- Our ultimate goal as a mom is to cultivate a strong and healthy family.

- Planning and organization are essential for becoming—and remaining—a strong family.

- God's will is for families to live for and glorify Him.

Moms, why should you want to organize yourself in order to build a strong family? Well, if you have babies, you will be better able to adapt to their crying, changing schedules, and sleep cycles if your day is well planned. If you have young children, you will have time to take them to their events, prepare meals, keep up with the housework and laundry, and be there for them emotionally. And, as you become better able to do for *them,* they will give back to *you* a more pleasant attitude and a willingness to be part of the family. If you have teenagers, good organization will allow you to be there for them, with love and acceptance, instead of criticism and frustration.

Ultimately, moms, the greatest benefit of becoming a more organized, stronger family comes when our children become adults. This is when we begin to reap all that we have sown. Your children can now be your friend, companion, and support. I would say that my two daughters are my very best friends in all the world.

---

*How far you go in life depends on your being tender with the young, compassionate with the aged, sympathetic with the striving, and tolerant of the weak and the strong. Because someday in life you will have been all of these.*

—George Washington Carver

---

 ## *Plan of Action*

For our twelfth and final step to becoming a more organized mom, we have emphasized how important it is to "Build a Strong Family." Where do you (and your husband, if you are married) want your family to go from here? What steps can you take to help your family become stronger in their relationship with God, with one another, and with their friends?

Look back at your response to Question #5 in the "Personal Inventory" section. Do you still agree with what you wrote, and the order of importance you gave your three ideas? If you do, then complete the sentence below by writing in your #1 choice. If your thinking has changed since reading this chapter, create a new #1 choice based on all that you've learned and thought about.

With God's help I want to _____.

I think I will have to change _____ in order to make this happen. I'm ready to step out in faith with God and make this change so that, with God's help, I can build a strong family.

Having come to the end of this book, think back to the times when you have seen either your own or another family reunited at an airport. Seeing each one jump up to greet their loved ones with a smile, a hug, maybe even a quick little dance, probably brought a smile to your face. A strong, loving family is a beautiful sight to behold, especially when the road today's families must travel is full of potholes and detours. Stay strong, dear mother! As you work to build character and faith in your children, you are shaping not only their future but also the future of our country. With God's help, you can do anything!

May God bless you as you become a more organized mom.

# Recommended Resources

With all the books, magazines, and websites available to us, I want to provide the names of some of my favorite resources. The books go into more detail, on many different subjects, than I was able to do in this book. Moms, I encourage you to read as much as you can. When we expand our thinking, we continue growing and becoming better moms.

## Books

Appleton, Nancy. *Lick the Sugar Habit.* Garden City Park, N.Y.: Avery, 1996.

Arterburn, Stephen. *Every Heart Restored.* Colorado Springs: Waterbrook, 2004.

———. *Every Heart Restored: A Wife's Guide to Healing in the Wake of a Husband's Sexual Sin.* Colorado Springs: Waterbrook, 2004.

Arthur, Kay. *God, How Can I Live?* Eugene, Ore.: Harvest House, 2004. Originally published under the title *Beloved.* Eugene, Ore.: Harvest House, 1994.

Barnes, Emilie. *Survival for Busy Women.* Eugene, Ore.: Harvest House, 1993.

Beausay, Bill. *Teenage Boys! Shaping the Man Inside.* Colorado Springs: Waterbrook, 2001.

Burkett, Larry and Rick Osborne. *Financial Parenting.* Chicago: Moody, 1999.

Cartmell, Todd. *Keep the Siblings, Lose the Rivalry: Ten Steps to Turn Your Kids into Teammates.* Grand Rapids, Mich.: Zondervan, 2003.

Chambers, Oswald. *My Utmost for His Highest.* New York: Dodd, Meade & Company, 1935.

———. *Daily Readings from My Utmost for His Highest.* Nashville: Nelson, 1993.

Chapman, Gary. *The Five Love Languages.* Chicago: Northfield, 1992.

Clinton, Tim, ed. *The Soul Care Bible.* Nashville: Nelson Bibles, 2001.

Colson, Charles. *Loving God.* Grand Rapids, Mich.: Zondervan, 1996.

Courtney, Vicki. *Your Girl.* Nashville: Broadman & Holman, 2004.

Covey, Stephen R. *The 7 Habits of Highly Effective Families: Building a Beautiful Family Culture in a Turbulent World.* New York: Golden Books, 1997.

De Graaf, John, David Wann, and Thomas H. Naylor *Affluenza: The All-Consuming Epidemic.* 2nd ed. San Francisco: Berrett-Koehler, 2005.

Dillow, Linda, and Lorraine Pintus. *Gift-Wrapped by God: Secret Answers to the Question, "Why Wait?"* Colorado Springs: Waterbrook, 2002.

Dobson, James. *Dare to Discipline.* Wheaton, Ill.: Tyndale, 1970. Rev. and repr. *The New Dare to Discipline,* Wheaton, Ill.: Tyndale, 1992.

———. *Home with a Heart: Encouragement for Families Preparing for Adolescence.* Wheaton, Ill.: Tyndale, 1996.

———. *The New Strong-Willed Child: Birth through Adolescence.* Wheaton, Ill.: Tyndale, 2004.

Elliot, Elisabeth. *Through Gates of Splendor.* New York: Harper, 1957.

Ethridge, Shannon. *Every Woman's Battle: God's Words of Encouragement to Guard Your Heart, Mind, and Body.* Colorado Springs: Waterbrook, 2005.

George, Elizabeth. *A Woman After God's Own Heart.* Eugene, Ore.: Harvest House, 1997.

Glenn, H. Stephen, and Jane Nelson. *Raising Self-Reliant Children in a Self-Indulgent World.* Roseville, Calif.: Prima, 2000.

Harley, Willard F., Jr. *His Needs, Her Needs: Five Steps to Romantic Love.* Grand Rapids, Mich.: Revell, 2002.

*The Holy Bible.* (There are many good English translations available. Find the one that works best for you.)

Huff, Priscilla Y. *101 Best Home-Based Businesses for Women.* Roseville, Calif.: Prima, 2002.

Hurnard, Hannah. *Hinds' Feet on High Places.* Shippensburg, Pa.: Destiny Image, 2003.

Jones, Stanton L., and Brenna B. Stanton. *How & When to Tell Your Kids about Sex: A Lifelong Approach to Shaping Your Child's Sexual Character.* Colorado Springs: NavPress, 1993.

Kelley, Linda. *Two Incomes and Still Broke?* New York: Times Books, 1996.

Kleiner, Susan M. *Power Eating.* 2nd ed. Champaign, Ill.: Human Kinetics, 2001.

Ladd, Karol. *A Positive Plan for Creating More Calm, Less Stress.* Nashville: W Publishing, 2005.

———. *The Power of a Positive Mom.* West Monroe, La.: Howard, 2001.

LaHaye, Tim, and Jerry Jenkins. *Left Behind* series. Wheaton, Ill.: Tyndale, 1996–2005.

Leman, Kevin. *Adolescence Isn't Terminal . . . It Just Feels Like It!* Wheaton, Ill.: Tyndale, 2002.

———. *The Birth Order Book: Why You Are the Way You Are.* Old Tappan, N.J.: Revell, 1985. Rev. *The New Birth Order Book.* Grand Rapids, Mich.: Revell, 1998.

———. *Making Children Mind Without Losing Yours.* Grand Rapids, Mich.: Revell, 2000.

———. *Running the Rapids.* Wheaton, Ill.: Tyndale, 2005.

Lewis, C. S. *The Chronicles of Narnia.* New York: HarperCollins, 2000.

———. *Mere Christianity.* London: HarperCollins, 1999.

———. *The Screwtape Letters.* London; New York: Collins, 1979.

Littauer, Florence. *Personality Plus.* Tarrytown, N.Y.: Revell, 1992.

Marshall, Catherine. *A Man Called Peter and the Prayers of Peter Marshall.* New York: Inspirational Press, 1996.

———. *Beyond Our Selves.* New York: McGraw-Hill, 1961. Repr. Grand Rapids, Mich.: Chosen Books, 2001.

———. *Something More.* Grand Rapids, Mich.: Chosen Books, 1996.

———. *To Live Again.* Carmel, N.Y.: Guideposts, 1990.

Maxwell, John C. *Today Matters: 12 Daily Practices to Guarantee Tomorrow's Success.* New York: Warner Faith, 2004.

McGraw, Phil. *Family First: Your Step-By-Step Plan for Creating a Phenomenal Family.* New York: Free Press, 2004.

Moore, Beth. *A Heart Like His: Intimate Reflections on the Life of David.* Nashville: Broadman & Holman, 1999.

———. *Praying God's Word: Breaking Free from Spiritual Strongholds.* Nashville: Broadman & Holman, 2000.

Nelson, Stephanie. *Greatest Secrets of the Coupon Mom.* Paramount, Calif.: DPL, 2005.

Omartian, Stormie. *The Power of a Praying Wife.* Eugene, Ore.: Harvest House, 1997.

———. *The Power of a Praying Parent.* Eugene, Ore.: Harvest House, 2005.

———. *The Prayer That Changes Everything.* Eugene, Ore.: Harvest House, 2005.

Osteen, Joel. *Your Best Life Now: 7 Steps to Living at Your Full Potential.* New York: Warner Faith, 2004.

Peterson, Eugene H. *The Message: The Bible in Contemporary Language.* Colorado Springs: NavPress, 2002.

Phillips, J. B., trans. *The New Testament in Modern English.* New York: Macmillan, 1988.

Point of Grace. *Girls of Grace: Devotional and Bible Study Workbook.* West Monroe, La.: Howard, 2002.

Pratt, Steven, and Kathy Matthews. *Superfoods RX: Fourteen Foods that Will Change Your Life.* New York: William Morrow, 2004.

RBC Ministries. *Our Daily Bread.* Ongoing devotional series. Grand Rapids, Mich.: RBC Ministries.

Schlessinger, Laura C. *The Proper Care and Feeding of Husbands.* New York: HarperCollins, 2004.

Stanley, Charles F. *When the Enemy Strikes: The Keys to Winning Your Spiritual Battles.* Nashville: Nelson, 2004.

Steward, H. Leighton, Morrison C. Bethea, Sam S. Andrews, and Luis A. Balart. *The New Sugar Busters! Cut Sugar to Trim Fat.* New York: Ballantine, 2003.

Swindoll, Charles R. *Getting Through the Tough Stuff: It's Always Something!* Nashville: W. Publishing, 2004.

——— *The Strong Family.* Grand Rapids, Mich.: Zondervan, 1994.

Ten Boom, Corrie. *The Hiding Place.* Boston: G. K. Hall, 1973. Repr. Grand Rapids, Mich.: Chosen Books, 1996.

Tobias, Andrew. *The Only Investment Guide You'll Ever Need.* Orlando, Fla.: Harcourt, 2005.

Warren, Rick. *The Purpose-Driven Life.* Grand Rapids, Mich.: Zondervan, 2002.

White, Joe. *Life Training: Devotions for Parents and Teens.* Wheaton, Ill.: Tyndale, 1998.

Wright, Bryant. *One Minute of Your Time: Right from My Heart.* Marietta, Ga.: Right from the Heart Ministries, 1997.

Yorkey, Mike, ed. *The Focus on the Family Guide to Growing a Healthy Home.* Brentwood, Tenn.: Wolgemuth & Hyatt, 1999.

Young, Ed. *Kid CEO: How to Keep Your Children from Running Your Life.* New York: Warner, 2004.

Ziglar, Zig. *Raising Positive Kids in a Negative World.* Nashville: Nelson, 2002.

## Other Recommended Authors

Jill Briscoe, John Eldredge, Ruth and Billy Graham, Anne Graham Lotz, David Jeremiah, Jan Karon, Beverly Lewis, Max Lucado, Peggy Noonan, Janette Oke, Eugenia Price, Helen Steiner Rice, Francine Rivers, Pat Robertson, Charles F. Stanley, Lee Strobel, Joni Eareckson Tada, Lisa Whelchel, Women of Faith, Philip Yancey.

## Bible Studies

Kay Arthur Bible Studies

Bible Study Fellowship studies

Blackaby, Henry. *Experiencing God.* Nashville: Broadman & Holman, 1994, 1997, 1998, 2002, 2004; Holman Bible Publishing, 1999. (Each year's book is published under a different title, but all begin with *Experiencing God.*)

Christian Woman's Club studies

Community Bible Study studies

Elizabeth George and Liz Curtis Higgs studies

Beth Moore Bible studies

Morgan, Elisa, and Carol Kuykendall. MOPS Bible Studies, such as "What Every Mom Needs: Balancing Your Life Workbook."

## Internet Resources

*http://quicken.intuit.com.* See where your money is going, and find ways to save with Quicken software.

*www.ChangeOne.com.* A great guide to healthy eating.

*www.cnb.com.* CBN National Counseling Center's "Guide to Financial Freedom" (also available by calling 1-800-759-0700).

*www.courageousparenting.org*

*www.focusonyourchild.com*

*www.healthywomen.org.* One-stop shopping for women's health. The National Women's Health Resource Center is the nation's leading independent, nonprofit organization specifically dedicated to educating women of all ages about health and wellness issues.

*www.mops.org.* A wonderful site for Mothers Of Preschoolers.

*www.onemillionmoms.com.* An online community of mothers dedicated to eliminating the exploitation of children.

*www.parentstv.org.* The conservative Parent Television Council (PTC) rates shows according to the level of violence, foul language, and sexual content. It also works toward requiring networks to move sexually explicit and violent shows to later time slots.

*www.pawsandtales.org.* A children's radio story time sponsored by Insight for Living.

*www.turbotax.com.* Buy *TurboTax* to submit your taxes online.

## Radio Broadcasts

*Adventures in Odyssey,* a radio program that broadcasts stories directed toward instilling values, morals, and godly character in children (from Focus on the Family).

## Family Camps

Pine Cove Christian Camps, in Tyler, Texas. Call 877-4PineCove.

Kanakuk-Kanakomo Kamps, in Branson, Missouri.